Sunset Cook Book of
SOUPS & STEWS

By the Editors of Sunset Magazine
and Sunset Books

Lane Books · Menlo Park, California

FOREWORD

"Soup of the evening, beautiful soup," reads a line in *Alice in Wonderland*. People often prefer simple soups and stews to fancier food, and these old favorites need not be reserved for the family, for guests also appreciate such honest fare. What could be more delicious than a hearty minestrone or savory lamb stew?

This book presents a marvelous array of soups and stews — substantial dishes for the family, lighter soups for lunch, first-course dinner soups, and festive soups and stews around which you can organize a whole evening's entertainment. Boiled dinners are also included, in which the meat and vegetables are simmered slowly in a flavorful broth (which then becomes a separate course). To expedite meal planning, fifteen complete menus are scattered throughout the book (see table of contents) featuring a soup or stew as the first course, the main dish, or an accompaniment for the meal.

You will soon notice from the classic recipes given in Chapter II that soups and stews can be quite dramatic. The special soup suppers in this chapter offer not only novel party ideas, but easy and often inexpensive ways to entertain.

Soups can be eaten anytime, during any course of a meal. Fruit soups make a sprightly dish for breakfast or an unusual dessert for dinner. Chilled soups supply the perfect answer for hot weather meals (and are delicious in winter, too). Refreshing to sip, cold soups are quite easy to prepare with a blender, the distinguished vichyssoise being a fine example.

A good soup or stew need not simmer for hours and hours. If time is limited, you'll find at your disposal recipes that can be prepared with canned and dried soups, giving them a home-style touch. Even many of the recipes which are made from scratch call for ready-made stock and cook in an hour or less. Those dishes which do cook for several hours usually require little attention.

If you love soup, but have never discovered borsch, pozole, gazpacho, and Mulligatawney, this book is at your service. And if stews have always made your mouth water, you will find here the world's favorites—goulash, ragout, ratatouille, curry, and hutsepot.

Cover photograph by Glenn Christiansen; recipe on page 20, Minestrone, Genoa Style. Illustrations by Bernice T. Glenn.

First Printing May 1967

CONTENTS

Menus

INTRODUCTION

What is a soup? What is a stew?

A certain comfortable air of informality pervades any meal in which the main dish is a soup or stew. And the mood is always more leisurely, more gracious when a meal begins with a soup. This book was designed to help you add these elements to both party and family meals.

Here, in considerable variety, are some of the world's classic soups and stews, each ideal for entertaining, often with dramatic staging. Here, also are soups to open your most luxurious meals.

For more day-to-day usage are the hearty but not too filling soups for lunch and supper (often quite quick to prepare) and the really substantial soups to make a meal upon; any of these would please unexpected guests. The same is true of the family-style stews in this book's collection.

HOW SOUPS AND STEWS DIFFER

A stew is a food that simmers or seethes gently in a liquid. It can be anything, but in the context of this book, it would be meat, fish, or poultry, and vegetables, with seasonings.

A soup can be a very wet stew, or simply the liquid that is flavored by the stewed ingredients.

The distinction between these two dishes is often difficult to make, for it is not at all uncommon to serve the cooked ingredients from a flavorful liquid

Golden colored Mulligatawney soup from India is pleasantly spiced; cooked rice and lemon slices are added to each bowl. Recipe on page 31.

as a stew, and also serve the broth as soup, right in the same meal. And, of course, you can serve either thick soup or well-sauced stew in a bowl to eat with a knife and fork.

The simplest soup is clear, well-flavored broth. (It is also one of the most satisfying low-calorie food choices for dieters.) In this category, bouillon, consommé, and stock are all pretty much the same; in fact, the terms are used interchangeably. All are water, seasoned by cooking with meat, poultry, or fish, with the optional addition of vegetables. The cook has great latitude as to the richness of flavor and inclusion of herbs and spices. The difference in canned broth, consommé, and bouillon is flavor; the names primarily are to help you remember which is which.

Broth becomes a more elaborate soup when you add a garnish such as avocado balls, toasted nuts, croutons, grated cheese, a spoonful of sour cream, or buttered popcorn. A good broth is also a suitable vehicle for various and sundry leftovers. Basic beef and chicken broths follow later in this chapter.

In addition to soups and stews based on broths, are those that start from scratch or incorporate step-saving convenience foods. Prepared soups and soup mixes are frequently called for to help reduce preparation time.

SERVING TEMPERATURES

A soup or stew, depending upon its character, should be served either steaming or frosty. A few are excellent either way, such as potato base vichyssoise and clam and tomato consommé bellevue.

To maintain the ideal temperature over a period of time, you will have to use such devices as electric warming trays; insulated serving containers (try an ice bucket for either hot or cold soups) or vacuum bottles for outdoor service; icers (bowls nested in cups filled with ice); ice right in the bowl as for Spain's gazpacho; candle warmers; electric bean pots; or chafing dishes. Sometimes it seems best to serve the soup or stew directly from the cooking pan at the stove or, perchance, at the fireplace hearth.

Such thermal precautions are necessary to preserve the best in flavor and consistency, particularly in meat-rich dishes that thicken or even congeal upon cooling — sometimes in your dish before you finish eating if the food was slightly cooled when served.

The refreshing nature of cold soups is absolutely dependent upon their being icy. But they should not be considered just hot weather dishes; try serving a cold soup before a hot, rich, or highly seasoned entrée; after an appetizer of these same qualities; with a hot sandwich or meat pie.

SERVING CONTAINERS

The esteem accorded soups in the world of fine cuisine is nowhere more apparent than in the astounding beauty, variety, and whimsey of the soup tureens which artists have created since cookery became civilized. Not all, of course, are masterpieces, but their capacious interiors are always adequate to their most important function as container from which to serve soup.

If you are without a venerable tureen, or just like more flexibility for presentation, look about your kitchen. Any handsome pot, bowl, or casserole will do if the size is appropriate. If the soup you are serving is of pouring consistency, a pitcher is a good dispenser. There are no fixed rules of etiquette to determine your choice. And the same freedom of choice applies to the bowls or equivalents from which you eat the soup. Deep ones are best for soups that cook quickly, such as a thin broth. Wide, shallow bowls suit thick, heat retaining soups and runny stews. Heatproof soufflé cups or ramekins are essential for soups with broiled or baked toppings. Cups or mugs are right for soups that you can sip, and so are pretty glasses and stemware.

WHEN TO SERVE SOUPS AND STEWS

Somewhere in this book is a soup or stew right for any occasion or setting. You will find some excellent dishes for outdoor meals which transport easily in sealed insulated containers. You can serve them from cups or paper bowls.

If you are a hostess who likes to accomplish a great deal before a party, soups and stews are ideal for entertaining; the decor or the accompaniments for a classic dish can establish a festive spirit.

For breakfast or brunch, a fruit soup or vegetable soup can be a logical addition. A fruit soup can also serve as a dessert or meal opener. Main-dish soups, in small portions, do as well as first-course soups. Stews retain their entrée nature at any meal, but it might be for lunch, supper, or dinner.

BASIC CHICKEN AND BEEF BROTHS

Many recipes in this book call for chicken or beef broth as the liquid base for a soup or stew. In most instances, you have the choice of using canned or freshly made broth; there are special points in favor of each.

Canned broths are easy to store, always ready to use, and keep indefinitely. However, canned broths, particularly those that are condensed, can't be reduced or boiled down for richer flavor concentration without becoming excessively salty.

In both of the basic home-cooked broths given here, salt is not added until you are ready to use it. At any earlier stage, you can, therefore, reduce the broth to the desired flavor level.

These broths freeze beautifully, and a constant supply is easy to maintain if you let the meat and bones simmer away on days when you will be in or near the kitchen for several hours. Large quantities of broth can be thawed quickly by warming in a pan over direct heat.

If you frequently make use of small portions of broth, why not freeze the liquid in ice cube trays, release the cubes, and store them in freezer bags?

Beef Broth

You roast the meat and bones first to develop a brown color in beef broth.

4 pounds cut up beef shanks and veal shanks
    (a mixture of these meats with flesh
    on the bones)
3 quarts water
2 carrots, cut in short lengths
2 medium-sized onions, each quartered
2 stalks celery
1 bay leaf
2 whole garlic cloves
2 whole cloves
4 to 6 whole black peppers
¼ teaspoon thyme
    Salt to taste when you use broth

Place shanks in a roasting pan and bake in a very hot oven (450°) for 20 to 25 minutes or until nicely browned. Transfer meats to a large pan and add water; rinse roasting pan well with some of the water to remove any browned particles and add to the large pan. Add to meat the carrots, onions, celery, bay leaf, garlic, cloves, peppers, and thyme. Bring to a boil and simmer, covered, for 2 hours. Pour broth through a wire strainer and reserve meat and vegetables for other uses only if their flavor is good. Cool broth; then chill.

To store in the refrigerator (no longer than 4 days), leave the fat layer on the surface until you are ready to use the broth; then lift the fat off and discard. To freeze, remove the congealed fat and transfer broth to freezer containers, allowing expansion room at the top of each container. Makes about 3 quarts.

Chicken Broth

5 pounds chicken backs, necks, and wings
½ cup chopped onion
1 sprig fresh parsley or ½ teaspoon dried parsley
1 bay leaf
¼ teaspoon thyme
⅛ teaspoon marjoram
3 quarts water
    Salt to taste when you use broth

Combine chicken, onion, parsley, bay leaf, thyme, marjoram, and water in a large deep pan. Cover and bring to boiling; then reduce heat and simmer for 3 hours or until meat falls readily from the bones. Pour broth through a wire strainer, discarding residue. Cool and chill, covered. To store in the refrigerator (no longer than 4 days), leave the fat layer on the surface until you are ready to use the broth; then lift the fat off and discard or save for other cooking uses. To freeze, remove the congealed fat and transfer broth to freezer containers, allowing expansion room at the top of each container. Makes 1½ to 2 quarts.

HOW TO CLARIFY BROTH

When making soups that consist of transparent broth with ingredients floating in the liquid, you can greatly enhance the appearance by first clarifying the broth to make it sparkling clear. The easiest method requires uncooked egg whites. In fact, this is a good use for those extra egg whites that often accumulate; you can freeze them until needed.

Bring broth to boiling. For each 1 quart of fat-free broth (freshly made or canned), whip 2 egg whites until frothy; then beat into the boiling liquid. Let mixture return to a rolling boil. Remove from heat and let stand until surface is calm.

Moisten a muslin cloth in cold water and wring dry. Line a wire strainer with the cloth and pour the hot liquid through it. Squeeze out liquid, taking care not to get any of the egg in the clear broth; discard egg whites.

If broth is still slightly murky, repeat the process with 2 more egg whites for each 1 quart broth.

FESTIVE SOUPS AND STEWS

Classic dishes from around the world

A few of the world's really great soups and stews are gathered together in this chapter. All are the prototype or the inspiration for some of our more prosaic, yet favorite everyday dishes. For example, Hungary's beef goulash is beef stew at a superb level; France's blanquette de veau is an exquisitely delicate veal stew; Italy's minestrone is a bean soup of infinite variation; Belgium's hutsepot is a boiled dinner with distinction.

Each of these classics is a main dish and automatically becomes the focal point of a menu. Since most of them are composed of meat and vegetables, very simple fare, such as bread, salad, and dessert, will complete a meal. Specific suggestions follow with many of the recipes.

Several of the soups — Spain's gazpacho and Italy's maritata — are of less substantial nature and, in small portions, could instead be served for a first course.

Mexican menudo is a soup with a remarkable range of flavors: To each bowl you add cool mint, green onions, and chile sauce. Recipe on page 27.

Preparation time for these soups and stews varies from just a few minutes to hours, but each involves steps that can be done ahead, or that require little attention over a long period of time. Most of your shopping can be limited to a well supplied supermarket, but occasionally you will have need of a good Italian delicatessen, or possibly an Oriental food market. Very often the unusual food items you seek will be used to complement the menu, rather than as a soup or stew ingredient.

One of the joys of presenting these dishes is the variety of settings they invite. These are the occasions to make use of your most decorative utensils and serving containers to emphasize the festive nature of the meal or the foreign origin of the menu. For example, if you happen to have a chimneyed cooker, use it for the Oriental friendship dishes. If you have marrow spoons, be sure to set them out with osso buco, for scooping the treasure from the heart of the veal bones. Shiny copperware or coarse red-brown French clay casseroles, with smooth glazed interiors, are well adapted to the service of onion soup, spring lamb stew, and similar entrées. Mexican pottery suitably honors the dishes pozole and menudo.

From France, Belgium, and Finland

Finnish Summer Soup

If you or a member of your family is a vegetable gardener, you must be familiar with the succulence and sweet flavor of tender young carrots, green beans, and tiny green peas. Finnish *kesäkeitto,* or summer soup, combines these choice ingredients in a rich, creamy broth to make an elegant main dish. Serve it for luncheon or supper, with crisp crackers or rye wafers and cold cuts. (If you haven't a vegetable garden, you can use frozen vegetables to replace the fresh ones.)

4 to 6 small new potatoes, peeled and halved
2 cups water
2 teaspoons salt
¼ teaspoon white pepper
2 tablespoons butter
4 tiny new onions, or 4 green onions cut in 3-inch lengths
16 very young (3-inch) fresh baby carrots, or 1 package (8 oz.) frozen whole baby carrots
2 cups fresh young snap beans, cut in 1-inch lengths, or 1 package (9 oz.) frozen cut green beans
2 cups fresh shelled tiny new peas, or 1 package (10 oz.) frozen petite green peas
2 cups half-and-half (half milk, half cream)
3 tablespoons flour

Cook the potatoes in simmering water for about 5 minutes (they should not be tender); add the salt, pepper, butter, onions, carrots, and green beans, and simmer 8 minutes more. Add the tiny green peas and cook another 2 minutes, or until the vegetables are tender crisp.

Mix together the cream and flour until smooth. Stir into the simmering vegetables, and cook about 5 minutes, stirring, until soup is thickened. Makes about 6 servings.

Basic French Onion Soup

French onion soup is one of the most celebrated in the world, yet its full possibilities are often overlooked. It makes an excellent entrée for a family supper or a fine conclusion to a late evening gathering. Embellished with freshly grated Gruyère and crusty sourdough bread, the rich beef broth and sweet onion rings make a substantial meal. All you need to add are a crisp green salad and a fresh fruit dessert.

This recipe should be served casserole style. Let it brew unattended in an ovenware pot until ready for its last-minute garnish.

6 large yellow onions, thinly sliced
2 tablespoons butter or margarine
1 tablespoon olive oil
6 cups freshly made or canned beef broth
⅓ cup white or red port or dry red wine (optional)
Salt and pepper to taste

Use a heavy-bottomed 3 or 4-quart covered pan. Sauté onions in butter and oil until limp. Cover and let simmer slowly for 15 minutes. Pour in beef broth or bouillon and wine (if desired) and simmer for 30 minutes. Or place in an ovenware casserole in a slow oven (300°) for 1 hour. Taste, and add salt and pepper if needed. Makes about 1½ quarts, or 6 servings.

A serving suggestion: Serve soup from the ovenware casserole or pour into a soup tureen; then ladle into individual bowls. Top each serving with a slice of buttered, dry-toasted French bread. (To prepare, slice French bread ½ inch thick, place on a baking sheet, and dry out in a moderately slow oven — 325° — for 20 to 25 minutes, or until lightly toasted.) Sprinkle each toast round with shredded Gruyère or Parmesan cheese and pass additional shredded cheese at the table.

Onion Soup Gratinée

A crust of bubbling cheese gilds this Paris market version of onion soup. Wholesalers, truckers, tourists, and a sprinkling of Parisian chic society consume countless bowls of it at dawn in the cafes of bustling Les Halles. You may wish to feature it as the entrée for a soup supper.

   Basic onion soup (recipe on page 10)
⅓ cup white or red port
½ cup diced Gruyère or Danish Samsoe cheese
 6 slices buttered, dry toasted French bread, sliced
        ½ inch thick (see recipe on page 10)
 1 cup mixed shredded Gruyère and Parmesan
        cheeses
 1 tablespoon melted butter

Make basic recipe of onion soup, omitting the wine. Pour lukewarm or cold soup and the port into an ovenproof earthenware casserole, cover, and heat in a moderate oven (350°) for 30 minutes.

Remove from oven and sprinkle with the diced Gruyère cheese. Cover with an even layer of toasted French bread and sprinkle with the shredded cheeses. Dribble over the melted butter. Return to a hot oven (425°) for 10 minutes, then turn on the broiler and heat just until the cheese browns lightly on top. Serve at once, ladled into soup bowls. Makes 6 servings.

French onion soup gratinée makes a full-meal supper dish, but in the bustling Central Market of Les Halles, Paris wholesalers, truckers, and tourists consume bowls of it in the early morning.

Hutsepot

The curly green cabbage in this version of *hutsepot* (pronounce it *hotsypot*), a popular meal in Belgium, reveals its origin in the North Sea province of Flanders. The name means foods combined in a cooking pot. The stock in which the foods are simmered is made into a quick pea soup and served as a first course.

3-pound boneless beef roast, tied (inside chuck
*   roll, cross rib, shoulder clod, rump, or*
*   sirloin tip)*
3 quarts water
4½-pound pork shoulder roast, boned and tied
*   (reserve bone)*
2 bay leaves
5 whole black peppers
1 tablespoon salt
8 small new potatoes
1 medium-sized head savoy cabbage
5 medium-sized white turnips
3 packages (10 oz. each) frozen peas
*   Toasted croutons*
*   Chopped chives*
*   Dijon-style mustard*
*   Prepared horse-radish*

Place beef roast in a large pan (at least 8-quart size); cover with the water. Heat to simmering. Simmer for 10 minutes; add pork and bone, bay leaves, and whole peppers. Bring to simmer again; skim foam from surface. Cover; simmer slowly until meats are just tender, 2½ to 3 hours, adding salt after meats have cooked for 1 hour.

Prepare and reserve vegetables: Wash potatoes, and peel a 1-inch band around center of each. Wash cabbage; trim and discard outer leaves, leaving as many of the firm, inner green leaves as possible. Trim end of core; cut cabbage into 6 or 8 wedges. Peel and quarter the turnips.

About 30 minutes before meat is done, add the turnips and potatoes; cook until just tender. (You can tie turnips and potatoes separately in cheesecloth for easy removal later.) Cook peas as directed on package until just tender; then drain and reserve.

Remove turnips, potatoes, beef, and pork from simmering liquid. Arrange the vegetables around the meat on a large, deep platter; cover platter with foil and keep warm. Strain the cooking liquid through several layers of cheesecloth. Remove 2 cups of the strained broth; reserve. Return remaining broth to pan. Add cabbage; simmer for 5 to 7 minutes or until just tender. Remove from cooking liquid; arrange on meat platter.

Meanwhile, put half of the cooked peas into blender container with 1 cup of the reserved broth; whirl until smooth. Press puréed peas through fine wire strainer, discarding pulp. Repeat with remaining peas and reserved broth. Stir strained peas into broth in pan; simmer until heated. Serve as a first-course soup, garnished with croutons and chives.

Then bring hot platter to table; slice meat to serve, accompanied by mustard and horse-radish. Makes 6 to 8 servings.

Pot au Feu

Pot au feu (translated from the French as "pot on the fire") is a lean beef pot roast cooked with leeks, carrots, and turnips. The cooking broth can be strained and served as a first-course soup.

About 1 pound cracked veal or beef
*   shank bones*
1 boneless beef rump roast, about 5 pounds
1 large onion
3 whole cloves
1 clove garlic
1 bay leaf
10 whole black peppers
3 sprigs parsley
1 teaspoon thyme
*   About 4 quarts water*
1 tablespoon salt
12 medium-sized carrots, whole
6 small turnips, whole
6 leeks, cut into 2-inch lengths
*   Toasted croutons or chopped chives (optional)*
*   Parsley or watercress for garnish*
*   Dijon-style mustard*
*   Horse-radish-flavored sour cream or whipped*
*   cream*

Pot au feu (literally "pot on the fire") is a simmered dinner made by cooking a beef rump roast with leeks, carrots, turnips, and herbs. The flavorful cooking broth forms the first course.

Arrange the bones in the bottom of a large pan (at least 6-quart size), and place the beef roast on the bones. Stud the onion with the cloves and put into the pan with the garlic, bay, whole peppers, parsley, and thyme. Add water to almost cover the meat, and heat to simmering point. Remove scum which forms on top; add ½ cup cold water, bring to a simmer again, then skim again. Keep doing this until the gray scum no longer forms—about 15 minutes.

Cover and regulate heat — or put into a moderately slow oven (325°)—so liquid continues to simmer very slowly until the meat is just fork tender, about 3 to 4 hours. Add salt after meat has cooked 1 hour. Later add the carrots, turnips, and leeks, allowing about 1 hour for the carrots and turnips to cook tender and about 30 minutes for the leeks to cook. (You might tie each kind of vegetable loosely in a piece of cheesecloth before you add it to the pot; then you can lift them out when perfectly tender and put them into a bowl with some of the broth. Just before serving, return to pot to reheat.)

To serve, lift out the meat, place it on a large, deep platter, and slice it. Arrange the vegetables around the meat. Cover platter with foil and keep warm until it is served. Strain the cooking liquid through several layers of cheesecloth and discard onion, cloves, garlic, and bay leaf.

Skim off the fat that has risen to the surface. Pour the broth into a soup tureen or individual dishes and garnish with toasted croutons or chopped chives, if you serve it as a first course.

Garnish the meat platter with parsley or watercress when you bring it to the table. Serve with the Dijon-style mustard or horse-radish-flavored sour cream or whipped cream. Makes 6 servings.

Navarin à la Printanière

This delectable French stew of lamb and vegetables holds a place of honor among the world's famous dishes, yet is a remarkably simple dish that adapts with ease to preparation in quantity. The recipe is proportioned to twenty servings and can be completely ready to serve an hour ahead of time.

10 pounds boned lamb shoulder (4 or 5 shoulder
  roasts)
3 tablespoons sugar
½ cup flour
1 tablespoon salt
4 cans (14 oz. each) beef broth
1 teaspoon rosemary, crumbled
2 bay leaves
  Hot cooked carrots, onions, turnips, potatoes,
    and yellow crookneck squash (directions
    follow)
2 packages (10 oz. each) frozen tiny peas, thawed

Trim excess fat from lamb and place fat in a large baking pan (such as a broiler pan bottom about 11 by 13 inches). Render fat in a very hot oven (500°) for 10 minutes, stirring occasionally.

Meanwhile cut lamb into about 2-inch cubes or chunks. Remove pan with fat from oven and measure 6 tablespoons of the fat and reserve; discard the remainder.

Mix fat with meat, then divide meat equally and place half in each of two large baking pans (the one in which the fat rendered and another of approximately the same size); spread meat out so that pieces are separated as much as possible and in a single layer. Sprinkle sugar evenly over the meat. Bake meat in the very hot oven (500°) for 20 minutes, uncovered, to draw the juices; stir several times. Alternate pan positions in the oven after the first 10 minutes.

Drain all juices from the meat and reserve. Mix flour with salt and sprinkle evenly over the meat, mixing to blend well. Return meat, uncovered, to the very hot oven and bake 20 minutes more, stirring occasionally. Alternate pan positions after the first 10 minutes.

During this time, boil the reserved pan juices until reduced to about 1 cup. Divide reduced liquid, the canned beef broth, rosemary, and bay leaves evenly between the 2 pans of meat, stirring free the browned particles in pans. Cover pans with close fitting lids or foil and bake in a moderately hot oven (375°) for about 1½ hours or until meat is very tender.

Gently transfer meat pieces to another container and pour the pan juices through a wire strainer to remove any lumps and most of the herbs (discard both bay leaves). Skim as much fat from juices as possible, then mix juices with meat. At this point you can refrigerate the meat, covered, overnight, then reheat and complete the dish the next day.

Unless you have a 7 or 8-quart (or larger) serving container in which you can cook, you will need to continue using the 2 baking pans (rinsed to remove all clinging particles) and divide meat and liquid between them. Cover and reheat in a slow oven (300°) for at least 1 hour, stirring occasionally. Then add all the cooked vegetables and heat, covered, for at least 1 hour or as long as 2 hours. An hour before serving, gently mix in the thawed peas. To serve, baste surface of the navarin with some of the juices to give it a fresh, shining look. Makes 20 servings.

HOT COOKED VEGETABLES:

You will need 20 carrots, 20 small boiling onions, 15 to 20 turnips, 20 very small potatoes, and 6 to 10 very small yellow crookneck squash. You can

French "springtime" stew (navarin à la printanière) will serve twenty people. Let the lamb simmer until tender in the oven; then add cooked potatoes, squash, carrots, turnips, onions, and peas.

cook the carrots, onions, and turnips the day before, but the potatoes have better flavor and the squash has better texture if not reheated.

Peel carrots, dividing each into thirds and trimming blunt ends to simulate tiny carrots. Peel turnips and cut any that are more than 1 inch in diameter into sections no thicker than an inch, trimming to make rounded shapes. Peel the onions.

Cook carrots, turnips, and onions separately in boiling salted water to cover in covered pans just until vegetables are easy to pierce; each requires about 15 minutes.

Drain well. Add to meat, or combine and cover with cold water; cover and refrigerate as long as overnight. Drain well, mix in with the meat, and heat as directed above.

Peel the potatoes and cook in boiling salted water to cover in a covered pan for 15 to 20 minutes or until easy to pierce. Keep in warm water until ready to add to stew (as long as an hour or two), then drain well and mix with meat.

Cut stem and blossom ends from squash and cut each in half lengthwise or into ½-inch-thick slices. Cook, covered, in boiling salted water to cover for about 8 minutes or until easy to pierce. Keep in warm water until ready to add to stew (as long as an hour; they can be held in the same container with the potatoes); drain well and mix with meat.

Blanquette de Veau

Brown stews are most familiar to American tastes, but the French are very fond of a creamy white veal stew, called *blanquette de veau*. It is not much more difficult to make than any other good meat stew, and except for the final thickening with egg yolks and cream, it can be made ahead for a company dinner.

Serve the blanquette with buttered noodles, white rice, or mashed potatoes, any of which might be arranged to encircle the veal and sauce on the serving plate.

2 tablespoons butter or margarine
2 pounds boneless veal shoulder, cut in 2-inch
    pieces

About 4 cups boiling water
1 veal bone, cracked
1 large carrot, cut in thick slices
1 medium-sized onion, quartered
2 parsley sprigs
½ bay leaf
2 sprigs fresh thyme or ½ teaspoon dried thyme
1 teaspoon salt
2 tablespoons butter
2 tablespoons flour
2 tablespoons lemon juice
2 egg yolks
⅓ cup heavy cream
    Salt, pepper, and lemon juice to taste
2 tablespoons minced parsley

Melt the 2 tablespoons butter in a large, heavy pan with a cover. Put in the veal pieces, cover the

A tender young rabbit is baked in a piquant, richly flavored cream for this company stew. The moist, fine-textured rabbit flesh lends itself admirably to the flavorful mustard sauce.

pan, and cook over low heat to let the meat release its juices — it shouldn't brown. Add boiling water to cover the meat, veal bone, carrot, onion, parsley, bay, thyme, and salt. Cover and simmer gently for 1¼ to 1½ hours or until the meat is tender.

Remove the meat pieces with a fork or slotted spoon and set aside. Strain the stock and discard bones and seasoning vegetables. Rinse the pan to remove any scum, pour in cooking stock, and boil rapidly until reduced to 2¼ to 2½ cups.

Using another pan, melt the 2 tablespoons butter; stir in the flour and cook, stirring, until bubbly. Remove from heat and gradually stir in the reduced cooking stock and the lemon juice. Cook, stirring, until the sauce is thickened and smooth, about 5 minutes. Combine the sauce and veal. This much can be done ahead and the dish refrigerated.

To serve, reheat the meat and sauce slowly just to the simmering point. Meanwhile, beat the egg yolks and cream together with a fork. Beat some of the hot sauce into egg mixture, then gradually stir back into the meat and sauce. Heat until sauce thickens slightly, but do not let the mixture boil. Add salt, pepper, and lemon juice, if needed. Garnish with parsley. Makes 4 or 5 servings.

Rabbit in Mustard Sauce

The elegant flavors blended in this classic French rabbit dish make it appropriate to serve on the grandest occasions. The stew is easy to prepare; butter-browned and brandy-flamed pieces of rabbit are baked in heavy cream that is prominently flavored by the delicate hot-tart tang of Dijon-style mustard.

2 fryer rabbits (each *about* 2½ *lbs.*), cut in serving pieces
  About 1½ teaspoons salt
  Flour
  About ½ cup (¼ lb.) butter or margarine
3 tablespoons warm brandy
½ cup minced green onion
¼ cup minced parsley
1 pound small whole or quartered large mushrooms
2 tablespoons Dijon-style mustard
2 cups heavy cream
2 tablespoons lemon juice
3 egg yolks, slightly beaten
  Chopped parsley

Sprinkle rabbit pieces with salt, then dust with flour, shaking off excess. Melt 5 to 6 tablespoons of the butter in a wide frying pan, and brown rabbit pieces, without crowding; place browned pieces in a 3½ to 4-quart casserole. To the last rabbit in the frying pan add the warm brandy and set afire. Place this rabbit and all juices in the casserole and keep warm.

Meanwhile cook the onion, parsley, and mushrooms in remaining butter (adding a little more if needed) until onion is soft, but not browned. Blend in the mustard, cream, and lemon juice and bring to a boil. Pour over the rabbit in the casserole. Cover and bake in a hot oven (375°) for about 45 to 55 minutes or until rabbit is tender enough to pierce easily.

Drain liquid into the wide frying pan and bring to boiling; boil rapidly 1 minute. Blend some of the hot liquid with egg yolks, then return mixture to pan. Cook, stirring constantly, until sauce is thickened; do not boil. Salt to taste. Pour sauce over rabbit, and sprinkle with chopped parsley. Makes 6 to 8 servings.

Some cooks like to keep a covered dish of ratatouille in the refrigerator for snacking. This French vegetable classic is easy to make, is good hot, cold, or reheated, and just about everyone likes it.

Ratatouille

COOK PEPPERS WITH ONIONS & GARLIC

Ratatouille is the rhythmic name of a delicious, freely formulated vegetable stew that originated along France's sunny southern coast. The appeal of making ratatouille ahead is enhanced by the fact that it tastes better after standing awhile.

    About ½ cup olive oil
    2 large onions, sliced
    2 large cloves garlic, minced or mashed
    1 medium-sized eggplant, cut in ½-inch cubes
    6 medium-sized zucchini, thickly sliced
    2 green or red bell peppers, seeded and cut in
        chunks
    About 2 teaspoons salt
    1 teaspoon basil
½ cup minced parsley
    4 large tomatoes, cut in chunks
        Parsley
        Sliced tomato (optional)

Heat ¼ cup of the oil in a large frying pan over high heat. Add onions and garlic and cook, stirring, until onions are soft but not browned. Stir in the eggplant, zucchini, peppers, 2 teaspoons salt, basil, and minced parsley; add a little of the oil as needed to keep the vegetables from sticking. Cover pan and cook over moderate heat for about 30 minutes; stir occasionally, using a large spatula and turning the vegetables to help preserve their shape. If mixture becomes quite soupy, remove cover to allow some of the moisture to escape.

Add the tomatoes to the vegetables in the pan and stir to blend. Also add more oil if vegetables are sticking. Cover and cook over moderate heat for 15 minutes; stir occasionally. Again, if mixture becomes quite soupy during this period, remove cover to allow moisture to evaporate. Ratatouille should have a little free liquid, but still be of a good spoon-and-serve consistency. Add more salt if required. Serve ratatouille hot; or cover, chill, and serve cold, or reheat to serve. Garnish with parsley and tomato. Makes 8 to 10 servings.

From Greece and Hungary

Beef Goulash

Any number of conglomerate mixtures are called by the name of goulash, but the authentic paprika-flavored stew of Hungary, *gulyás,* has a distinctive personality of its own. To be sure, there is no one recipe for goulash, nor is there perfect accord as to what makes a goulash. But a good goulash differs from "just any stew" in this way: Chunks of good meat brown slowly, as does a quantity of onions. The seasoning is the sweet Hungarian paprika, if available (look for it in gourmet food shops; you can use regular paprika for good tasting, but quite different results). Then the stew, in any further variations, simmers to tenderness in liquid.

Commercial sour cream might be passed at the table for each person to add and stir into his serving, or you can blend about ½ cup of the sour cream into the meat sauce just before serving.

    4 pounds boneless beef chuck, cut in 1½-inch
        cubes
      About 1 cup water or all or part dry red wine
    2 tablespoons bacon drippings or butter
    6 medium-sized onions, chopped
    3 tablespoons Hungarian paprika
1½ teaspoons salt
    1 or 2 green peppers, coarsely chopped
        (optional)

Using a heavy frying pan *and* a heavy pan or Dutch oven and dividing the meat between them, brown meat in its own fat slowly and thoroughly on all sides. Transfer browned meat cubes in the frying pan to the Dutch oven; rinse the frying pan with 1 cup water and add to meat. Cover Dutch oven and start to simmer meat.

Meanwhile heat drippings or butter in the frying pan; add onions and cook slowly, stirring often, until lightly browned. Stir in paprika and salt, and add to meat with green pepper, if used. Continue cooking, slowly, without letting it boil, for 2 to 3 hours, or until meat is very tender, not soft. Add more liquid if needed during cooking, but it should not be soupy. Taste and add more salt, if needed. Goulash is equally good reheated. Makes 8 to 12 servings.

If you like, add potatoes: Peel and cut 4 to 6 medium-sized potatoes into eighths. Add to the meat about 30 minutes before it is done and cook until both meat and potatoes are tender.

Szekely Gulyás

Next to beef, the Hungarians favor pork for making goulash. This version with pork, sauerkraut, and sour cream originated in the eastern part of old Hungary, Transylvania (now Romania). Typical accompaniments are dark bread and cold beer.

    2 large onions, finely chopped
    2 tablespoons butter or margarine
    2 pounds lean pork shoulder, cut in 1-inch cubes
    1 teaspoon salt
    3 teaspoons Hungarian paprika
    1 teaspoon caraway seed
        About 1 cup water
    2 cans (about 1 lb. each) sauerkraut, drained
    1 cup commercial sour cream

In a large, heavy frying pan or Dutch oven, slowly sauté onion in butter just until onion is transparent. Add pork, sprinkle it with salt, and slowly sauté, stirring to brown well on all sides. Stir in paprika and caraway seed. Add ¼ cup of the water, cover pan, and simmer slowly, stirring occasionally, until meat is tender, about 45 minutes. (Add more water as needed, but no more than ¼ cup at a time.) Stir in sauerkraut and simmer about 15 minutes longer. Taste, and correct seasoning, if needed. Stir in sour cream, and as soon as it is heated through, serve. Makes about 8 servings.

Avgolemono

Avgo (eggs) and *lemono* (lemon juice) are the basis of this low calorie Greek specialty. Be sure to use low heat, once you combine the ingredients, to prevent curdling of the eggs.

4 cups rich chicken broth (canned, freshly made, or made with 4 cups water and 3 tablespoons chicken stock base)
4 eggs
4 tablespoons lemon juice
1 whole lemon, thinly sliced

Heat chicken broth to boiling. Beat eggs until light and foamy and beat in the lemon juice. Gradually stir in part of the hot broth, beating constantly. Return to the pan with broth and place over very low heat, stirring, until soup is thickened. Pour into small cups or bowls and garnish each with a lemon slice. Makes 6 to 8 first-course servings.

Chicken Lemon Soup

Make avgolemono soup as directed on this page, but add 3 tablespoons instant cooking rice to the boiling broth; remove from heat and let stand 5 minutes. Pour part of the hot broth into the beaten eggs and lemon juice and return to pan. Add 1 can (5 oz.) boned chicken, flaked; heat, stirring, until soup is thickened. Serve in bowls and float a lemon slice in each serving. Makes 4 servings.

From Italy

Minestrone, Genoa Style

Minestrone, a sustaining vegetable soup, is part of the way of life in Italy. Every cook has an individual way with minestrone; generally, the common characteristic is beans, fresh or dried, or both.

4 quarts water
1 pound ham
1 pound bony chicken parts
¼ pound sliced prosciutto or bacon
2 cups diced potato
2 cups sliced celery
4 small zucchini, sliced in ½-inch pieces
  About 1½ cups sliced leeks
1 pound Italian (Romano) green beans, cut in 2 to 3-inch lengths
½ cup salad macaroni (ditalini)
1 pound peas, shelled
3 to 4 cups shredded white cabbage
  About 2 teaspoons salt
  Pesto sauce (recipe follows)

Combine water, ham, chicken, and prosciutto, and bring to boiling. Cover and simmer 2 hours. Strain and reserve stock; discard meat and bones. Bring stock to boiling and add potatoes; cover and simmer 10 minutes. Remove cover and add celery, zucchini, leeks, green beans, and macaroni and simmer 5 minutes. Stir in peas and cabbage and cook 4 or 5 minutes more. Salt to taste. Ladle soup at once into bowls (the green vegetables lose their bright color if allowed to stand) and spoon in Pesto sauce to taste. Makes 6 to 7 quarts.

PESTO SAUCE:

Combine in a blender ¼ cup chopped parsley, 1 cup fresh basil leaves or ¼ cup of the dried herb, 1 cup freshly grated Parmesan cheese, and whirl, adding 6 to 8 tablespoons olive oil until a smooth thick paste is formed. Or you can mash these ingredients to a smooth paste in a mortar and pestle. Then add 2 tablespoons of lemon juice. Makes about 1 cup.

⊙⊙⊙

Minestrone, North Beach Style

This savory thick version of minestrone is a favorite in San Francisco's North Beach area.

STOCK:

1 pound cranberry (or pink) beans
4 quarts water
4 marrow beef bones, each 3 inches long
4 slices meaty beef shank, each 1 inch thick

COOKED VEGETABLES:

4 tablespoons olive oil or salad oil
2 large onions, diced
2 cups diced carrots
2 cups diced celery
2 cups diced leeks
1 can (1 lb.) solid pack tomatoes
   About 2 teaspoons salt

RAW VEGETABLES:

2 or 3 large potatoes, diced
2 cups (½ lb.) green beans, cut in 2-inch pieces
4 small zucchini, sliced
3 cups shredded white cabbage
½ cup salad macaroni (ditalini)
½ cup chopped parsley
1 clove garlic, minced
2 tablespoons dried basil
2 tablespoons olive oil
   Grated Parmesan cheese

First prepare the stock as follows: Cover the cranberry beans with the water and bring to a boil. Boil 2 minutes; remove from heat and let stand, covered, for 1 hour. Add the marrow beef bones and beef shank slices; bring to boiling and simmer for 2 hours. Let cool; remove meat and bones from beans; return lean meat to soup if flavor is good. Scoop marrow from bones and add to soup; discard bones. Mash half the beans by rubbing through a wire strainer, or whirl in a blender with some of the liquid. Return to whole beans in pan.

Next, prepare cooked vegetables. Heat the 4 tablespoons olive oil or salad oil in a wide frying pan. Add the diced onions and cook until soft. Then add the diced carrots, celery, and leeks; cook for 5 minutes over medium heat. Mix in the tomatoes, mashing slightly. Simmer rapidly for 10 minutes or until most of the liquid has evaporated. Add to the prepared bean stock; bring mixture to boiling and simmer for 30 minutes. Season with the salt.

The raw vegetables are added at this point. To the boiling soup, stir in the diced potatoes and cut green beans. Simmer rapidly, uncovered, for 10 minutes; then add sliced zucchini, shredded white cabbage, and salad macaroni. Simmer 5 minutes more. In another pan, sauté the chopped parsley, minced garlic, and dried basil in the 2 tablespoons olive oil until parsley is bright green. Mix into soup and serve. Sprinkle grated Parmesan cheese into each bowl. Makes 6 to 7 quarts.

A happy marriage of flavors, the rich stock of maritata soup is swirled with a cheese-butter-egg-cream mixture, and then returned to the bowl. You can prepare this exceptional dish right at the table.

Maritata Soup

Maritata, in Italian, means married; it is also an exceptional soup. Delightfully easy to prepare, maritata has showmanship potential in its making. If you like, you can prepare it right at the table in a chafing dish.

First, cook a few thin strands of noodles in a rich broth; then add a velvety mixture of sweet butter, Parmesan cheese, egg yolks, and thick cream (blended in the kitchen), literally whipping it all together before your guests. The few ingredients group easily on a large tray.

While the noodles cook, serve a salad such as Belgian endive with a tart dressing. Offer crusty bread with the soup as the main course, and end with baked winter pears, sugared strawberries, or fresh summer melon, depending upon the season.

6 cups hot rich meat broth (all chicken, all beef, or combination of these, freshly made or canned)
2 ounces (⅛ of a 1-lb. package) vermicelli noodles
½ cup (¼ lb.) soft sweet (unsalted) butter
¾ cup freshly grated Parmesan cheese
4 egg yolks
1 cup heavy cream

Bring broth to boiling over direct heat (on a range top or over a denatured alcohol flame). Add vermicelli noodles (broken, if desired) and cook, uncovered, for 5 to 8 minutes or until noodles are tender to bite.

In a bowl blend the sweet butter with cheese and egg yolks, then gradually beat in the cream. (If you cook at the table, prepare this mixture in the kitchen.) Spoon a small amount of the hot broth into the cream mixture, stirring constantly; then pour this mixture back into the hot broth, stirring constantly. Immediately extinguish heat, if using a chafing dish, or remove from heat. Ladle soup into bowls, including some of the vermicelli. Makes 4 to 6 main-dish servings (or 8 to 10 first-course portions).

Beef and Sausage Rapallo

Rapallo, where this dish originated, is a small town near Genoa in northern Italy. The recipe's name simply means beef boiled (but really simmered) with coteghino (a sausage) as done in Rapallo. The stock in which the meat and vegetables cook is made into a smooth chive sauce to pour over the meat.

You may have to order the coteghino from an Italian delicatessen; the seasonings in this sausage flavor the brisket, vegetables, and sauce. Leftover meats are good thinly sliced and reheated in a little butter.

About 5-pound piece fresh beef brisket
2 to 3 quarts water or meat broth (canned or
  freshly made)
1 carrot
1 medium-sized onion
1 celery stalk
3 or 4 parsley sprigs
1 bay leaf
8 to 10 whole black peppers
4 to 6 whole allspice
  Salt
1 coteghino sausage (1 to 1½ lbs.)
3 to 4 large carrots, each peeled and cut in half
6 to 8 small whole potatoes, scrubbed but not
  peeled
6 to 8 small, whole, boiling-sized onions
3 to 4 large stalks celery, each cut in half
  Chive sauce (recipe follows)

Put the brisket in a large baking pan and bake in a very hot oven (500°) for 35 minutes; turn meat over after the first 25 minutes (add 3 or 4 tablespoons water to pan if drippings begin to char). Transfer brisket to a large deep kettle, and rinse roasting pan with some of the water or broth to free all the browned particles. Cover meat with this liquid plus enough more to total 2 to 3 quarts.

Add to pan the carrot, onion, celery stalk, parsley, bay leaf, black peppers, allspice, and 2 teaspoons salt (if cooking liquid has none). Bring to a boil, immediately reduce heat to a gentle simmer, and cover pan. Cook for about 3 hours; meat should feel slightly tender when pierced. Add the coteghino sausage and continue to simmer for 1 more hour.

Remove brisket and sausage from broth and keep in a warm place (such as a 200° oven) while you make sauce and cook remaining vegetables. Strain and measure 2 cups of the broth; reserve for the chive sauce.

Bring remaining broth in pan to boiling. Add carrot halves, potatoes, and boiling onions; cook, uncovered, for 15 minutes. Add the celery; cook for another 5 minutes. Remove vegetables from broth with a slotted spoon. (Refrigerate this broth for soups or other uses.) Slice brisket and coteghino; arrange on warm platter with vegetables. Serve the chive sauce separately to pour over meat. Makes 6 to 8 generous servings.

CHIVE SAUCE:

Cook 1 tablespoon minced shallots or green onions in 1 tablespoon butter over medium heat until soft but not browned. Blend in 2 tablespoons flour; gradually add 2 cups strained cooking liquid. Simmer gently for about 10 minutes, stirring occasionally. Blend in 4 to 6 tablespoons minced chives (fresh, freeze-dried, or frozen) and 2 to 4 tablespoons half-and-half (half milk, half cream).

Osso Buco *(see suggested menu below)*

Osso buco (OH-so BOO-koh) translates descriptively as marrow bones, the main ingredient in this Italian stew. A fanciful eating tool called a marrow spoon is the traditional implement used to scoop out the fragile succulent marrow, although a small demitasse coffee spoon will do; if there is no other choice, use a knife tip.

When you order the meat, be sure to specify exactly what you need — meaty sections of the veal shank that also contain marrow.

Italian Dinner

Green Salad
Osso Buco *(see recipe above)*
Tiny Buttered Peas   Butter-Browned Mushrooms
Boiled Small Whole Potatoes
Italian Bread
Rosé or Chablis
Tortoni Cups

Introduce this meal with a salad of crisp romaine with a garlic-flavored oil and vinegar dressing, and such embellishments as fried croutons, slivers of salami, marinated artichokes, and cherry tomato halves.

The combination of tiny buttered peas, butter-browned mushrooms, and small whole potatoes is excellent with the tender veal and rich marrow, especially when you drizzle them with the osso buco sauce.

Any crusty loaf, perhaps sweet or sour Italian bread, is appropriate with the osso buco. The wine might be Grenache Rosé or a Chablis, such as Pinot Blanc or Pinot Chardonnay. For dessert, a simplified version of biscuit tortoni waits in your freezer until just before you want to serve it.

TORTONI CUPS

2 cups almond macaroon crumbs, firmly packed
1 cup apricot jam or peach jam
1 quart slightly softened toasted almond ice cream
1 cup heavy cream, whipped
    Red and green candied cherries

Combine the macaroon crumbs and the apricot or peach jam and mix with a fork until the crumbs are coated with jam. Spread the crumb mixture evenly over the bottoms of the tortoni cups (8 to 16 paper cup-cake liners or ceramic cups, depending on their size). Cover crumbs with the slightly softened ice cream. Top with swirls of the whipped cream. (Instead of using individual cups, you can layer the ingredients into a 1½-quart casserole with straight or sloping sides and cut in wedges to serve.) Decorate attractively with the candied cherries. Cover lightly with waxed paper. Put in the freezer until the cream has frozen stiff. Then cover well with heavy foil and freeze until needed. Remove from freezer about 5 minutes before serving. Makes 8 to 16 servings.

7 to 8 pounds meaty slices of veal shank with
    marrow in the bone, cut in 2-inch-thick
    slices (12 to 18 pieces)
  Salt and flour
6 tablespoons butter
1½ cups dry white wine
 ¾ to 1½ cups chicken broth (canned or
    freshly made)
1½ tablespoons grated lemon peel
 ½ cup minced parsley
  1 medium-sized clove garlic, mashed

Sprinkle shanks with salt, then roll in flour, shaking off excess. Melt butter in a very large heavy pan and brown shanks on all sides; remove browned pieces from pan to prevent crowding. Return all meat to pan, add wine and ¾ cup of the broth, and simmer, covered, gently for 2 to 2½ hours or until meat is tender; add more broth if sauce becomes too thick. (If you cook the meat uncovered, the liquids will reduce rapidly, making an even more flavorful sauce, but you must check frequently to avoid cooking the meat dry. You can cook meat the day before, cool, cover and refrigerate overnight. Reheat slowly for 30 to 45 minutes before serving.)

Carefully remove meat to a warm platter (keep sections whole) and put in a warm place. Bring sauce to a rolling boil, scraping free browned particles; add a little more broth if needed to keep liquid. Mix lemon peel, parsley, and garlic. Add half this mixture to sauce and let simmer several minutes; garnish meat with remaining lemon peel mixture. Salt to taste. Pour sauce over the meat, or serve separately to ladle on as desired. Makes 6 to 8 servings.

Osso buco is a superlative Italian version of stew. Dig the tender treasure of marrow from the veal shanks with a special utensil called a marrow spoon, or use a demitasse coffee spoon.

From Mexico, Spain, and Brazil

Red Spanish Gazpacho

One of the warmest regions of Spain is Andalusia, home of a dish exceptionally suited to warm weather dining — *gazpacho*. When served icy cold, gazpacho is best described as a cooling salad in soup form. It makes an excellent main course for lunch, with hard rolls, a rich or sharp cheese, and a favorite dessert.

> 1 medium-sized sweet onion, coarsely chopped
> 2 medium-sized cucumbers, peeled and coarsely
>   chopped
> 4 large tomatoes, peeled and coarsely chopped,
>   saving all juice
> 1 small clove garlic
> 1 can (4 oz.) pimientos
> 3 cups cold water
> 3 tablespoons red wine vinegar
>   About 2 teaspoons salt
> 1 cup fine dry bread crumbs or 1½ cups croutons
> ¼ cup olive oil
> 2 tablespoons olive oil (optional)
> 1 medium-sized sweet onion, chopped
> 1 medium-sized cucumber, unpeeled and diced
> 2 or 3 large tomatoes, peeled and chopped, saving
>   juice
>   Ice cubes

Combine in a blender the coarsely chopped sweet onion, the peeled cucumbers, the 4 tomatoes, garlic, and pimientos; whirl until fairly smooth, or grind vegetables through the fine blade of a food chopper. Blend vegetables with cold water, vinegar, and salt. You can thicken this soup with bread crumbs or serve it with croutons sprinkled in each bowl. If you use the crumbs, heat the ¼ cup olive oil in a frying pan; add the crumbs and stir until richly toasted. Blend with soup.

If you prefer the croutons, heat the ¼ cup olive oil in the frying pan; add the croutons and stir until toasted. Reserve for adding to the soup when serving. In this case, add the 2 tablespoons olive oil to the soup.

Chill soup thoroughly. To serve, ladle into bowls; have ready in small bowls the chopped sweet onion, the unpeeled and diced cucumber, 2 or 3 tomatoes (peeled and chopped, with juice), the croutons (unless you added bread to the soup), and ice cubes. Add some of each of these condiments to each bowl. Makes 6 servings.

White Spanish Gazpacho

Cucumbers make the base of this gazpacho white; chopped tomatoes, parsley, onions, and almonds are added later. Rest the serving bowls in ice for perfect eating temperature. Bread and dessert are all that you need to complete the menu for a luncheon or supper.

3 medium-sized cucumbers, peeled and
   cut in chunks
1 small clove garlic
3 cups chicken broth (canned or freshly made)
3 cups commercial sour cream
3 tablespoons white vinegar
  About 2 teaspoons salt
4 medium-sized tomatoes, peeled and chopped
½ cup chopped parsley
½ cup sliced green onions
¾ cup toasted salted whole almonds

Combine the cucumbers and garlic in a blender. Have ready the chicken broth and sour cream. Whirl cucumbers and garlic until smooth with a little of the chicken broth; then blend cucumber mixture with the remaining broth. Stir a little of this mixture into the sour cream; then stir into the cucumber liquid (or grind cucumbers and garlic through the fine blade of food chopper and mix with broth and sour cream). Season with white vinegar and salt to taste. Cover and chill.

To serve the soup, ladle into wide shallow bowls and, if possible, nest each bowl in crushed ice. Have ready in small bowls the tomatoes, parsley, green onions, and almonds. Spoon these foods, as desired, into soup bowls. Makes 6 servings.

Menudo

Mexican menudo (mey-NOO-doh) is a soup with a remarkable range of flavors. It contains quantities of beef, hominy, and tripe, and is enriched by both spices and herbs — cinnamon, cloves, oregano. To each bowl, you add the widely contrasting tastes of cool mint (fresh or dried), warm green onions, and hot chile sauce. Start this dish a day ahead to allow time for flavors to blend.

Warm tortillas are the natural accompaniment. Before dinner, serve foods you can eat with your fingers — empanadas (small pastry turnovers filled perhaps with a savory meat mixture), guacamole (the avocado sauce) with tostadas, or miniature tamales. For dessert, serve soft jack cheese, sliced, with quince paste (available in Mexican food specialty shops).

2 pounds tripe, cut in slivers
3 quarts water
  About 2 teaspoons salt
4 pounds thick meaty slices beef shank
4 large onions, chopped
2 whole cloves garlic
3 cans (1 lb. each) golden hominy, drained
1 teaspoon oregano
2 cinnamon sticks, each 3 inches long
8 whole cloves
  Relishes (see below)

Put tripe into a deep pot; add water and 1½ teaspoons of the salt. Bring to a boil and simmer, covered, for 2 hours. Add beef, onion, garlic, hominy, oregano, cinnamon, and cloves. Simmer 2½ hours more. Cool, cover, and chill overnight.

Skim off fat and discard shank bone and connective tissue. Cut meat in pieces and return to soup. Simmer 30 minutes; salt to taste. Ladle into large individual bowls, adding 1 or 2 tablespoons of each relish to every serving. Makes 8 to 10 servings.

RELISHES:

In separate containers, offer the following: 1 to 1½ cups sliced green onions (tops included), 1 to 1½ cups chopped fresh mint (or 1 cup dried mint), and 1 to 1½ cups canned red chile sauce, green chile salsa, or tacos sauce.

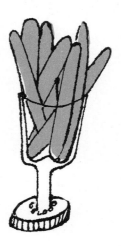

Pozole

Of the many different versions of Mexico's Pozole, all contain pork (often a pig's head) and either hominy or corn. This version is made from inexpensive pork hocks (the meaty ends cut from the hind legs of fresh pork); the result is a very flavorful broth that is full of meat.

To serve the soup, have at the table an assortment of chopped fresh vegetables (such as lettuce, radishes, green onions, carrots, avocado), cubes of cream cheese or other soft cheese, if you like, and, without fail, wedges of lime. The vegetables and cheese are spooned into the piping hot soup, and the lime is squeezed in to taste by each person.

Crunchy corn sticks made from a corn muffin mix and baked in corn-stick pans might be served with this soup; follow it with a favorite make-ahead dessert of your own choosing.

2 large fresh pork hocks, split in 2 or 3 pieces each
2 quarts water
1 can (1 lb.) solid pack tomatoes
2 cans (1 lb. each) hominy, drained
2 medium-sized onions, finely chopped
4 teaspoons salt
  Chopped fresh vegetables and cheese
    (suggestions at left)
2 limes, cut in wedges
  Liquid hot-pepper seasoning (optional)
  Prepared horse-radish (optional)

Black beans are flavored by smoked beef tongue, ham, sausage, and bacon in Feijoada, a hearty Brazilian dish. Fresh orange chunks provide an unusual accent; toasted farina tops each serving.

Put the pork hocks into a large kettle with the water, tomatoes, hominy, onions, and salt. Simmer for 2 to 3 hours, or until the meat begins to come away from the bones. Remove pork hocks from soup; cool both meat and soup. Remove meat from the hocks, discarding fat and bones; cut the meat into small pieces. When the soup is cold, skim off the fat. Just before serving, add meat to soup and heat, adding additional salt if needed. Serve with an assortment of chopped fresh vegetables, and with lime wedges; you might also provide liquid hot-pepper seasoning and prepared horse-radish for those who prefer hotter seasonings. Makes 8 to 10 servings.

Feijoada

Black beans with rice are staple fare in Brazil, and one of the most popular dishes is made by boiling the beans with smoked beef tongue, ham, sausage, and bacon. The smoky flavors of the meat permeate the beans and are deliciously accented by peeled and quartered oranges that are added near the end of the cooking time. It is a hearty dish with robust flavors that appeal especially to men.

A Brazilian wouldn't think of eating *feijoada* (fay-ZHWA-da) without spooning it over hot rice and sprinkling manioc meal on top. However, your guests may prefer the beans without rice. Manioc meal is not readily available in the United States, but farina cereal, toasted in a heavy frying pan, makes a good substitute (stir over medium heat until an even light brown). Black beans are available here in many Oriental and Mexican markets, or you can use ordinary pink beans.

Sour French bread is good with this dish. You might follow the main course with fruit salad to double as salad and dessert.

    4 cups black beans or pink beans
      Cold water
    1 smoked beef tongue
¾ to 1 pound linguisa (Portuguese-type sausage)
    1 pound smoked pork butt or ham
½ pound unsliced bacon
    2 medium-sized onions, finely chopped
    1 clove garlic, minced or mashed
    1 bay leaf
¼ cup chopped parsley
      Peel from half an orange
    3 navel oranges (peel and all white membrane cut
        off)
      Cornstarch (if necessary)
      Salt
      Rice (optional)
1 cup toasted farina

Soak the beans overnight in cold water to cover. (Or, instead of the overnight soaking, cover beans with water and bring to a boil; boil 2 minutes, remove from heat, and allow to soak 1 hour.) Rinse and drain; put beans into a large kettle with a tight-fitting lid. Add 6 cups cold water to the beans. Cover and simmer gently for about 2 hours.

Meanwhile cook the tongue; simmer in water to cover until tender (about 2 hours), peel, then slice. Pre-cook sausages in simmering water for about 30 minutes; cut each into 3 or 4 pieces. Cut the ham into 1-inch cubes and the bacon into ½-inch cubes. Add all the meats to the beans. At the same time add the onion, garlic, bay leaf, parsley, and orange peel. Continue to cook slowly, adding water as needed to keep the liquid just above the level of the beans, until the beans are tender (about 6 hours). About ½ hour before the cooking is complete, add the peeled oranges, which have been cut into quarters. The mixture should be thick; if not, thicken with cornstarch, diluted first with a little water to make a paste. Add salt to taste; remove orange peel. Makes about 12 servings.

From India, Japan, and China

Lamb Curry

Check your spice supply before starting this curry, but don't be concerned that it will turn out too spicy. The dish has a smooth exotic flavor and an extra bonus — your kitchen will be filled with a delicious aroma all the time it cooks. If your market doesn't carry ground coriander, you can buy whole coriander seed and grind it with a mortar and pestle. The yogurt base loses its identity, but contributes an interesting tart flavor to the sauce.

You'll want to serve the curry on hot cooked rice and offer several condiments such as a Major Grey chutney, salted cashews, and the yogurt relish that follows. Tea or beer is a typical beverage companion to a curry. For dessert, you might consider pineapple sherbet or fresh fruits, and almond cookies.

```
 2 medium-sized onions
 2 cloves garlic
 2 tablespoons ground coriander
 2 teaspoons salt
 2 teaspoons cumin seed
1½ teaspoons black pepper
1½ teaspoons ground cloves
1½ teaspoons ground cardamom
 1 teaspoon ground ginger
 1 teaspoon ground cinnamon
 1 teaspoon poppy seed
 ⅓ cup lemon juice
 2 cups yogurt
 5 pounds boneless lamb, cut in 1½-inch cubes
 ¼ cup (⅛ lb.) butter
    Curry powder (optional)
    Yogurt relish (directions follow)
```

Cut 1 of the onions and 1 clove of the garlic directly into an electric blender. (If you don't have a blender, grate the onion and mash the garlic and combine in a bowl.) Add the coriander, salt, cumin, pepper, cloves, cardamom, ginger, cinnamon, poppy seed, and lemon juice; whirl or beat until smooth and thoroughly blended. Blend in the yogurt. Pour this sauce over the meat in a large container, stirring until all the meat pieces are coated. Cover and let stand 1 to 2 hours at room temperature, or overnight in the refrigerator.

Melt the butter in a large frying pan or other heavy pan; thinly slice the remaining onion and 1 clove of garlic, and sauté in the butter until golden. Add the meat, including the marinating sauce. Cover and simmer slowly until the lamb is tender, about 2 hours. This makes quite a mild curry, so taste and add prepared curry powder (we used about 3 teaspoons) if you want to increase the curry spiciness. Makes about 12 servings.

YOGURT RELISH:

Blend 3 cups yogurt with ¼ cup finely chopped green onion, 1 teaspoon salt, 1 teaspoon sugar, and 1 tablespoon ground cumin. Remove stem ends from 4 small zucchini or peel 2 cucumbers. Shred the vegetable and add to yogurt. Chill, covered, until ready to serve.

Mulligatawney Soup

This golden colored soup comes from northern India. Served in wide shallow bowls to allow room for adding cooked rice, Mulligatawney is ideal for informal entertaining. With it, you need only a crisp salad of greens, bread, and a light dessert. For the bread you might serve the crisp Indian wafers called *papars,* which are made by simply frying quickly in hot oil the prepared *pappadums* that are now available in most specialty food stores. Still another possibility is to serve crisp, fried flour tortillas, which are similar to some Indian breads.

2 broiler-fryer chickens (2 to 3 pounds each) or
    1 chicken plus 2 legs and thighs, cut in serving pieces
2 quarts water
1 tablespoon salt
½ cup (¼ lb.) butter or margarine
4½ teaspoons powdered turmeric
3 tablespoons poppy seed
3 tablespoons ground coriander, or whole coriander seeds, crushed
    Dash cayenne
½ cup packaged grated coconut or flaked coconut
1 medium-sized onion, finely chopped
3 to 4 cloves garlic, minced or mashed
1 cup flour or rice flour
1 can (1 lb.) garbanzo beans
4 or 5 whole cloves
    Additional salt and cayenne pepper to taste
    Hot cooked rice
    Lemon slices

Put all the chicken, including the bony pieces, into a large pan (about 4-quart). Add water and salt; bring to a boil; cover and simmer for 45 minutes to 1 hour, or until chicken is tender. Remove chicken pieces; cool slightly; then carefully remove meat from backs, wings, and breast. Cut breasts into 3 or 4 pieces each; leave legs and thighs whole. Discard all the meat-free bones and reserve chicken stock.

In the same large pan, melt 6 tablespoons of the butter. Add turmeric, poppy seed, coriander, cayenne, coconut, onion, and garlic; cook together about 5 minutes, or until onions are soft. Remove from heat and stir in flour. Add the garbanzo beans, which have been whirled smooth with their own liquid in the blender (or rubbed through a fine strainer). Gradually stir in the reserved chicken stock; simmer together about 15 minutes, stirring frequently. Add the chicken pieces.

Just before serving, melt the remaining 2 tablespoons butter with the cloves; remove cloves and stir butter into soup. Taste and add additional salt and cayenne pepper, if needed. Serve in large soup bowls; at the table, pass hot cooked rice and lemon slices to be added by each guest. Makes about 8 generous servings.

Beef Mizutaki

In the Orient, a meal centered on one dramatic dish, cooked and served at the table, is known as a friendship dish. Guests share from a communal cooking pot, around which they are congenially grouped at a small table. This idea adapts well to more general entertaining, for the following two friendship dishes from Japan and China are appetizing by any standard. The dishes are individually suited to accommodate only 4 to 6 guests, but you can duplicate the service at another table if you want to serve a greater number.

The ingredients, cooked, raw, or partially cooked, may be artfully arranged for cooking, or already assembled in the cooking container. Broth is the cooking medium. You can do almost everything well ahead of mealtime.

The cooking device may be anything from an electric frying pan to a flameproof container over a portable heat source, such as an alcohol flame or hibachi, to the chimneyed oriental cooker that is made for the friendship dish. Whatever you use, be sure the container is securely seated above the heat and the heat is steady and low, yet hot enough to keep the broth simmering. The chimneyed oriental cookers should never be heated without liquid in the cooking moat; otherwise you may damage the cooker. Fill the chimney halfway with well ignited charcoal and close the moat with its cover top during cooking. Be sure that the metal lining of the moat is one which is safe for cooking, and not just for ornamental use. [*Continued on page 32*]

Mizutaki is one of the most familiar friendship dishes because restaurants in Japan and a few on the West Coast have popularized this Japanese peasant dish. The traditional name, which comes from *mizu* (water) and *taki* (to cook), describes the dish: Meat and a selection of vegetables are cooked in water or stock, then dipped in a delicious sesame seed sauce as they are eaten.

Begin the meal with hot sake (Japanese rice wine) and a selection of dainty Japanese morsels such as pickled shrimp, smoked oysters, red caviar, or sliced broiled mushrooms. Serve hot rice with the mizutaki, if you wish. For dessert, offer small bowls of mandarin orange sections mixed with chunks of pineapple and flavored with candied ginger. When the meal is over, you might pass to each guest, on a miniature plate, a small towel wrung out in hot water and twisted dry.

COOKING LIQUID:

You can prepare broth well in advance of your party. Combine in a large kettle 4 thick slices of beef shank, 2½ quarts water, 2 celery tops, 1 quartered medium-sized onion, 2 teaspoons salt, and 6 whole black peppers; cover and simmer for about 2 hours. Strain and refrigerate until needed. If you prefer, use 3 cans (10½ oz. *each*) condensed beef broth with enough water to make 2 quarts liquid.

INGREDIENTS FOR TABLE COOKING:

You can cut and arrange the meat and vegetables several hours before your party; keep the plates well covered with saran film and in the refrigerator. As with sukiyaki, ingredients for this dish may be added or subtracted at will; they are listed in order

of their importance. (If you use less variety than suggested here, increase quantities of ingredients accordingly.)

*2 to 3 pounds lean beef (sirloin or tenderloin),
    sliced paper thin*
1 bunch Chinese cabbage
1 pound spinach
2 medium-sized onions
2 or 3 Japanese eggplants or ½ regular eggplant
½ pound fresh mushrooms
1 can (8 oz.) bamboo shoots
1 or 2 green peppers
2 or 3 carrots
2 or 3 stalks celery
2 cakes soy bean curd (tofu), optional

You might have your meat man run the beef through his slicing machine; cut each thin slice into strips about 1 inch wide. There's a choice of ways to present the cabbage and spinach; the Japanese way is to roll them together into medallions as follows: Separate leaves from the Chinese cabbage, cut out tough stem sections, and blanch in boiling water to make pliable. Arrange a layer of cabbage on a sheet of waxed paper. (Layer should be about 7 inches wide and 8 or 16 inches long — making either one long roll or two shorter ones.) Remove tough stems from the spinach; blanch in boiling water just until limp; drain and stack to form a cylinder down middle of cabbage leaves. Roll up tightly by lifting waxed paper and slipping the paper from the roll as you form it. Gently squeeze in an absorbent towel to remove excess liquid; remove from the towel. Holding the roll securely, cut with a sharp knife into 1-inch thick slices.

An alternate way to prepare these two vegetables is to cut the whole head of Chinese cabbage in even diagonal slices about ½ inch thick. After removing the tough stems, carefully stack each 5 or 6 leaves of the spinach and cut each stack in 2 or 3 diagonal slices.

Cut the onions in half vertically, then thinly slice each half diagonally. Slice eggplant about ¼ inch thick. Thinly slice mushrooms. Slice the bamboo shoots thinly; if large, cut each slice in several pieces. Remove stems and seeds from green peppers; thinly slice. Cut carrots in thin diagonal slices, or cut ridges into 4 sides of carrots and slice to make flower patterns. Slice celery diagonally. Cut tofu into ½-inch cubes. Arrange each of the ingredients attractively on a separate dish, or arrange several compatibly colored ingredients on the same tray.

SAUCE:

This type of sauce made with sesame seed is called *goma* in Japan; it is used in this recipe for dipping the meat and vegetables. Finely ground peanut butter makes a satisfactory substitute for all or part of the sesame seed (use about ⅔ cup peanut butter for the total amount of sesame seed).

> 1 cup (about 6 oz.) sesame seed
> ½ cup salad oil or sesame oil
> ½ cup soy sauce
> 2 tablespoons rice vinegar or lemon juice
> ¾ cup beef broth (canned or freshly made) or
>   water

Toast the sesame seed in a dry frying pan over medium heat, stirring to brown the seeds evenly. Grind until fine and slightly pasty in consistency (use high speed in an electric blender, or grind a few at a time with a mortar and pestle). Thoroughly blend the ground seeds with salad oil, soy sauce, vinegar, and beef broth. The sauce will be quite thick, but each person can dilute his portion to taste with some additional broth from the cooking pot—it should be about the consistency of heavy cream.

For a spicier sauce, cut thin rings from 1 or 2 dried hot red chiles; heat in 1 tablespoon salad oil and add (cautiously) to taste. Garlic can also be added to taste.

CONDIMENTS:

These are all optional, but are nice to have on the table for each guest to add to his bowl of sauce —finely minced green onions; shredded fresh ginger; and Japanese chile powder, a mixture containing hot chiles, powdered orange peel, black sesame seed, and other seasonings. The chile powder is available in Japanese markets; it's hot and should be used sparingly. If you can find it, we suggest you have this condiment on the table instead of adding hot chiles to the sauce when you make it.

SETTING THE TABLE:

Set each place at the table with a small plate, a pair of chopsticks, a fork, napkin, and a small bowl of the sauce. You may also want at each place a cup for tea, a bowl for drinking the broth, and a tiny sake cup. Near the cooking pot you will need a ladle for the broth and a slotted spoon for removing the cooked meat and vegetables.

PROCEDURE FOR COOKING AT THE TABLE:

Bring the cooking pot to the table with about half of the hot broth (1 quart); surround it with the foods ready to be cooked. From this point, there are two different ways to approach the cooking, depending partly upon how adept your guests are with chopsticks. The traditional way is to pass the dishes of food, each guest taking onto his plate some of each. Using chopsticks, each puts his own meat and vegetables into the simmering broth and, when done to his liking, removes them to his plate, then dips each morsel in sauce as he eats it. Sometimes they cook one thing at a time, sometimes several. Either way it's a long and leisurely repast.

For a faster start to this meal, the hostess can put into the pot about half of each of the ingredients, keeping foods as separate from each other as possible, cover the pan, and let the ingredients cook for about 5 minutes. Then guests lift out onto their plates some of each food (the hostess might also assist by serving some of the cooked foods onto plates).

Either way, it is customary halfway through the dinner to ladle out the hot stock — now richly flavored with meat and vegetables — and drink it. Then the whole process is repeated, but for the second soup-drinking, have each guest mix the broth into his remaining dipping sauce to make a rich, invigorating soup. Makes 4 to 6 servings.

Chrysanthemum Bowl

The most elaborate of all the Chinese common-pot dishes is the chrysanthemum bowl. In China, this dish is the feature of a ceremony presided over by the hostess.

During the ceremony, vegetables and a variety of meats are cooked and served at the table. When all the foods have been eaten, a rather dramatic finale is performed. The hostess drops chrysanthemum petals into the steaming broth, thus adding a surprisingly spicy and delicious flavor to the soup. Each guest further enriches his portion by cooking an egg in the broth.

The recipe given here will serve six people generously. Rice and green tea are traditionally served with this meal. Although the Chinese seldom use a dipping sauce, several condiments are suggested that enhance the flavor of the dish. To conclude, you might pass a plate of Chinese confections, such as candied coconut strips, preserved ginger, and candied fruits or peels. Fortune cookies would also be in order.

COOKING LIQUID:

You can prepare this the day before your dinner. Start with a large broiler-fryer chicken (about 4 pounds); carefully remove the breast and reserve. Cut up the remaining chicken and put into a large pot with 2½ quarts water and ¼ cup of soy sauce. Bring to a boil and simmer about 1 hour. Cool, and strain the stock (use the cooked chicken meat for a salad or casserole); refrigerate stock until needed.

INGREDIENTS FOR TABLE COOKING:

You can do all the necessary cooking, cutting, and arranging of these foods several hours in advance; cover and refrigerate.

1 whole chicken breast (or 2; you may want to
    buy an extra whole breast)
1 to 2 pounds spinach
½ head Chinese cabbage
1 pound white firm-fleshed fish, such as halibut
    or swordfish
1 cup small oysters
½ pound peeled, deveined, jumbo shrimp or
    prawns
½ pound pork tenderloin
½ pound chicken livers or 2 pork kidneys
    (optional)
¼ pound bean thread (optional; see below)
    Salad oil for frying (optional)
2 large white chrysanthemum blossoms
6 raw eggs

Slice the chicken breast very thin. Remove tough stems from the spinach; stack each 5 or 6 leaves together, then cut in 3 or 4 diagonal slices. Slice the cabbage diagonally about 1½ inches wide. Slice fish. Leave oysters whole. Cut each shrimp in several pieces. Slice pork very thin. Blanch the chicken livers or kidneys and slice thin.

If you include the bean thread, be sure to buy the right kind. It is called *saifun* by the Chinese, *harasume* by the Japanese. Another type, which looks the same, is called *shirataki,* but it turns into a sticky dough instead of puffing up when fried. Fry the bean threads in deep fat heated to 390°; they will immediately puff up and turn white in a rather explosive fashion (try out a few strands first, so that you will be prepared); remove and drain. Arrange each of the above ingredients attractively in bowls or trays. Wash the blossoms well. Leave eggs in shells.

CONDIMENTS:

These are optional. The nicest way to serve them would be in miniature dishes (such as those sold inexpensively in Chinese and Japanese shops) at

After all the foods have been cooked and eaten, the Chinese chrysanthemum bowl concludes dramatically as the hostess plucks blossoms into the richly flavored broth. Each guest cooks an egg in the broth.

each guest's place. You might also serve soy sauce, oyster sauce (available in Chinese and Japanese markets), and minced green onion. You may prefer to dilute the oyster sauce with some of the broth until the consistency of cream and serve in small bowls as a dipping sauce, as suggested for mizutaki on pages 31-33.

SETTING THE TABLE:

Set each place with a small plate, chopsticks, fork, napkin, rice bowl, tea cup, and a cup for drinking the broth. Also include tiny dishes of the condiments, if used. Each guest gets one of the uncooked eggs. Near the cooker you'll need a ladle, a slotted spoon, and the chrysanthemum blossoms.

PROCEDURE FOR COOKING AT THE TABLE:

Bring the cooking pot to the table with about half of the chicken stock; surround it with the dishes of food to be cooked. Meanwhile serve the hot rice. Follow the same procedure for cooking as described for mizutaki, on pages 31-33. The cooked foods can be dished onto individual plates or directly into each guest's rice bowl.

When all the foods have been cooked, add the flower petals to the rich remaining stock. Each guest can then either beat an egg in his bowl and ladle some of the hot stock over it, or—and this is a real trick—break his egg into the common pot, poach it, and remove it to his plate with chopsticks. (We suggest you have a slotted spoon or "leaking ladle," as the Chinese call it.) Makes 6 servings.

SOUPS TO START A MEAL

Prelude to a special dinner

A meal that begins with soup is, by its nature, one of elegance and greater formality, since the meal must be presented in courses. You can temper the mood as you like, however, by the way in which you serve the soup: in cups for guests to sip before they adjourn to the dinner table (perhaps going by a buffet table where the entrée awaits); in cups or bowls filled from a tureen or a pitcher at the table; or in bowls already in place when guests are seated.

Most soups in this chapter are surprisingly quick to make and require few ingredients. Some are to be served hot, others chilled, and several jellied. The soups are grouped according to their consistency and richness (or at least the illusion of richness). First you will find the flavored and garnished broths. Here beef and chicken broths are basic ingredients; usually you have the choice of using broth that is freshly made (see page 7), canned, or made from stock concentrate or bouillon cubes. Be sure to dilute canned condensed broths according to label directions if the recipe

Ladle this delicately flavored lobster-zucchini soup into deep bowls and offer hot boiled rice to add to the soup. Recipe on pages 40-41.

does not specify condensed broth. These lean, but extremely flavorful soups, such as wine consommé or orange-beef broth, are perfect introductions to lavish main dishes or to meals where you wish to keep the overall calorie total low.

Next come the soups that derive their overt flavor and sometimes their velvety texture from vegetables and usually cream in some form (sour, heavy, whipped). A group of shellfish soups overlaps into this category. Typical ingredients are convenience foods that you can always have on hand.

To speed the assembly of a good number of these soups, an electric blender is almost indispensable. Lacking it, however, you'll find reliable but slower results are possible with a food mill or a fine wire strainer and elbow power.

Cream and purée soups are in such great variety that you're sure to find the right flavor to complement any menu. Scaled for service in small portions, ideally they do not satiate the appetite, but hone it for what is to follow.

A final category includes the fruit soups. In the European tradition, a fruit soup can begin or end a meal. You might serve one for breakfast in place of a less inspired fruit dish, or for lunch. Many fruit soups are limited to their service by season, but those made with canned or frozen fruits can bring a touch of spring and summer lightness to any meal, any time of the year.

Broths

Lemon Consommé

Precede fillet of sole or other delicate fish dishes with lemon-scented consommé.

Add ½ teaspoon grated lemon peel and 2 tablespoons lemon juice to 3 cups boiling chicken broth (freshly made, canned, or made with chicken stock concentrate). Garnish each serving with lemon slices. Makes 4 or 5 servings.

Lime Consommé

Light and refreshingly fragrant, lime consommé is particularly pleasant as an introduction to a Mexican or curry dinner.

Bring 3 cups chicken broth (freshly made, canned, or made with chicken stock concentrate) to a boil. Add ¼ teaspoon grated lime peel and 2 tablespoons lime juice. Float a thin slice of lime in each serving. Makes 4 or 5 servings.

Sherried Beef Consommé

Sherried beef consommé makes a fine accent for a roast beef menu. Bring 2 cups canned beef consommé and 1 cup water to a boil. Add 1 tablespoon sherry; cover and reduce heat. Let simmer 1 or 2 minutes. Pass shredded sharp Cheddar cheese to sprinkle over servings. Makes 4 or 5 servings.

Wine Consommé

A dry red wine such as Cabernet or Zinfandel perfumes classic beef consommé. The liquid is clarified with egg white to give it sparkling clarity; serve the soup hot, or jellied, cold.

4 cups beef broth (canned, freshly made, or made with beef stock concentrate)
1 egg white, slightly beaten
1 cup dry red wine
1 teaspoon sugar
  Dash lemon juice
  Salt and pepper
  Thin lemon slices

Heat beef broth to boiling point. To clarify it, stir in the egg white, and bring mixture to a boil. Pour soup through a moistened muslin cloth; discard egg white and return clarified broth to the pan. Bring again to a boil and add wine, sugar, and lemon juice. Add salt and pepper to taste. Serve hot, garnished with lemon slices. Makes 6 servings, about ¾ cup each.

JELLIED WINE CONSOMMÉ:

Soften 2 envelopes (about 2 teaspoons *each*) unflavored gelatin in ½ cup water. Add gelatin mixture to boiling clarified broth (see above), along with wine, sugar, and lemon juice; chill until set. Whip with a fork and serve with lemon wedges.

Consommé Bellevue

Two ingredients that you can keep on hand at all times—tomato and clam juices—are the constituents of a zestful cocktail-like soup.

Combine equal parts canned tomato juice and clam juice. Season with a dash of liquid hot-pepper seasoning and a little lemon juice. Serve hot or cold. To serve jellied, add 2 teaspoons unflavored gelatin, softened in ¼ cup cold water, to each pint of the hot soup. Chill and serve in cups.

Mushroom-Tarragon Bouillon

This clear broth is best served piping hot, perhaps in cups to sip. It can be prepared ahead and frozen.

1 pound mushrooms
5 cans (10½ oz. each) beef bouillon
3 soup cans water
2 teaspoons dried tarragon
Salt and pepper
¼ cup sherry (optional)

Finely mince mushrooms or put through food chopper with medium blade. Combine mushrooms with bouillon and water; simmer for 30 minutes, adding the tarragon the last 10 minutes. Pour through a moistened muslin cloth. Discard mushrooms. Correct seasoning and add the sherry, if desired. Reheat and serve from a tureen; keep warm on an electric warming tray or over a candle. Makes 12 servings.

Orange-Beef Broth

There's a subtle flavor and aroma of orange in this clear beef broth. Serve in cups or mugs with a twist of orange.

2 large navel oranges
3 tablespoons butter or margarine
2 cans (10½ oz. each) beef broth
1 soup can water
½ cup orange juice
1 teaspoon sugar
2 whole cloves

Using a vegetable peeler, cut thin strips about an inch long of orange zest (only the colored layer of the skin); cut one for each serving of soup and set aside to use for garnish. With a sharp knife, cut all the remaining peel, including the white membrane, from the oranges. Lift out the orange sections (work over a pan to catch all the juices); discard the pulp and peel. Add butter to the orange sections in the pan and simmer for about 3 minutes.

Add the beef broth, water, orange juice, sugar, and cloves. Bring to a boil and simmer about 10 minutes. Press through a wire strainer (cool and refrigerate if you make this soup ahead).

Reheat the clear broth just before serving. Pour into cups or small soup bowls, adding a twist of the reserved orange peel to each cup. Serve piping hot. Makes 6 servings.

Madrilène

Chilled madrilène makes a colorful beginning for a company dinner in any season. With it, you might wish to serve crisp buttered bread fingers or heated melba toast and a lemon wedge garnish.

Chill 2 cans (12 oz. *each*) madrilène for 4 hours or until set. Turn madrilène out into a bowl and break up with a fork; spoon into chilled bouillon cups or bowls. Top each portion with a dollop of commercial sour cream, finely minced chives, and freshly ground black pepper. Center a small spoonful of red caviar in each mound of sour cream. Makes 4 to 6 servings.

Almond Soup

Delicate chicken or shellfish is complemented by almond soup. Add ¼ cup light cream and ¼ teaspoon almond extract to 3 cups boiling chicken broth (freshly made or canned). Serve immediately. Float a brightly colored flower, such as bougainvillea, in each bowl. Makes 4 or 5 servings.

Green Chile Soup

Peanut butter and chiles give an Indonesian character to this soup. It makes a refreshing introduction to a grilled halibut or salmon dinner.

Remove seeds and pith from canned green California chiles and mince enough to make 1 tablespoon. Blend chile with 3 tablespoons chunk-style peanut butter, 1 tablespoon tomato catsup, and 3 cups chicken broth (freshly made or canned). Heat to boiling; sprinkle with a dash of cayenne and serve hot. Makes 4 or 5 servings.

Spanish Garlic Soup

Spanish garlic soup will remind you of the classic French onion soup, but the clear broth makes it lighter. The garlic flavor is distinct, but not harsh.

10 cloves garlic, peeled and sliced
¼ cup olive oil
 5 cups beef broth (canned or freshly made)
 1 cup dry sherry
   Salt and pepper
   Toasted sliced French bread
   Shredded Parmesan cheese

Sauté garlic in oil until golden. Heat broth with sherry; when broth reaches the boiling point, add garlic with oil. Season with salt and pepper to taste, and simmer for about 30 minutes. Strain out the garlic and reheat. To serve, sprinkle the toast slices generously with cheese, and place them in a hot oven (425°) for about 3 minutes. Place toast in soup dishes, and pour in soup. Makes 4 servings, each of 1-cup size.

Tortilla Soup

The parched corn flavor of tortillas flavors this simple broth soup.

3 corn tortillas, cut in thin strips
  Salad oil
4 cups chicken broth (freshly made, canned, or
    made from chicken stock concentrate)
1 medium-sized tomato, chopped
4 green onions, chopped with part of the tops
  Grated Parmesan cheese

Sauté the tortilla strips until crisp in a wide frying pan containing about ⅛ inch hot salad oil. Drain strips on paper towels. Bring to a boil the chicken stock with the chopped tomato and onion and the tortilla strips. Simmer slowly 15 or 20 minutes. Top each serving with grated Parmesan cheese. Makes 4 servings.

Chinese Watercress Soup

Slivers of green onion, water chestnut, and celery mingle with nippy watercress in an easily assembled Oriental-style soup.

 4 cups chicken broth (freshly made, canned, or
     made from chicken stock concentrate)
 3 tablespoons shredded cooked lean pork
 ¼ cup finely sliced celery, cut on the diagonal
 ¼ cup sliced water chestnuts or bamboo shoots
 2 green onions, thinly sliced on the diagonal
 1 tablespoon soy sauce
 1 cup watercress leaves, packed

Combine chicken broth, pork, celery, water chestnuts or bamboo shoots, green onions, and soy sauce; bring to boiling. Simmer for 5 minutes; add watercress and serve hot. Makes 6 servings.

Lobster Soup

This soup from the Philippines is made with frozen lobster; have it cut in half when you buy it. Offer hot boiled rice to add to each serving if you want a more substantial dish.

*1 frozen rock lobster tail (about 8 oz.), cut in half
    lengthwise*
2 tablespoons butter or margarine
6 cups chicken broth (canned or freshly made)
*1 cup thin noodles, such as broken vermicelli or
    small egg noodles*
1 small zucchini (about 4 inches long), thinly sliced
2 eggs, beaten
    Salt and pepper
    Hot cooked rice (optional)

Sauté the cut surface of frozen lobster in butter for about 1 minute. Add the broth and quickly bring to a boil. Lift lobster from soup and set aside. Stir noodles and zucchini into soup and let simmer for about 3 minutes, or until noodles are tender. Meanwhile, remove lobster meat from shell and cut in chunks. When noodles are cooked, return lobster meat to soup. Pour eggs in a thin stream into the soup, swirling broth as you do so. Season with salt and pepper to taste. Ladle soup into bowls, and add a spoonful of hot rice to each serving, if desired. Makes 6 to 8 servings.

Egg Drop Soup

Clear Chinese soup with swirl of egg is complemented by thin wheat wafers.

In a pan, dissolve 4 chicken bouillon cubes in 4 cups hot water; add 1 cup diced raw tomato and simmer for 5 minutes. Beat 1 egg slightly; add to the soup; then stir constantly 1 or 2 minutes, or until the egg separates in shreds. Serve at once. Makes 4 to 6 servings.

Try this formula for Spanish garlic soup: Ladle hot sherried beef stock, liberally seasoned with garlic, over thick slices of toasted French bread which have been topped with Parmesan cheese.

Beef Soup with Liver Dumplings

In Viennese tradition, hot beef soup with liver dumplings would be served at the table in soup plates as the first course; Wiener schnitzel might be the main dish.

½ pound beef or calf liver
3 slices white bread, crusts removed
  Water
2 tablespoons finely chopped onion
2 tablespoons bacon drippings or butter
1 teaspoon finely chopped parsley
1 egg
  Dash each salt, pepper, and marjoram
¼ to ½ cup fine dry bread crumbs
1½ quarts freshly made beef broth or 2 or 3 cans
    (10½ oz. each) beef consommé
  Finely chopped parsley (optional)

First prepare the dumplings: Cut liver in pieces and whirl in the blender or put through a meat chopper with a fine blade. Soak the bread in a little water; then squeeze as dry as possible. Put bread into blender with liver and whirl, or put the liver and bread again through the meat chopper. In a small frying pan, sauté the onion in the bacon drippings or butter until golden; add parsley and leave a minute or two over the heat; then remove. Combine the liver and bread with the onion mixture. Add the egg, salt, pepper, marjoram, and ¼ cup of the bread crumbs, adding more bread crumbs until mixture is a consistency you can form into soft walnut-sized balls with two teaspoons. You can cover the bowl at this point and refrigerate the dumpling mixture until time to heat the soup.

To serve, heat your own beef broth or the canned consommé, diluted with an equal amount of water, until it is boiling. Spoon in the dumpling mixture, cover, reduce heat, and simmer for 6 minutes. Sprinkle a little finely chopped parsley on each serving of soup. Makes 6 servings.

Creams and Purées

Carrot Soup

Ladle pretty orange-colored carrot soup into bowls or mugs and lightly dust each individual serving with nutmeg.

4 pounds bony chicken pieces (backs, wings, necks)
6 or 8 sprigs parsley
10 or 12 carrots, peeled
2 large onions, sliced
  About 2 teaspoons salt
8 cups water
1 cup heavy cream
  About ¼ teaspoon nutmeg

Tie chicken and parsley in a bag formed from a single thickness of cheesecloth. Place in a deep pot. Add carrots, onions, 1½ teaspoons of the salt, and the water. Cover, bring to a boil, and simmer slowly for 2 hours. Cool slightly; lift bag from broth and drain well. Discard bones and parsley.

Remove carrots and onions from broth with a slotted spoon and whirl in a blender with some of the broth, about 2 cups at a time, until smooth (or force through a wire sieve). Return vegetable purée to broth in pan; stir in cream, ¼ teaspoon of the nutmeg, and additional salt if needed. (You can do this much a day ahead and chill soup, covered, overnight.) Heat to simmering and serve; sprinkle each portion with nutmeg. Makes 12 to 13 cups or 10 to 12 servings.

Cream of Lettuce with Roquefort

Roquefort adds a piquant touch to the cream topping of the soup recipe given here.

4 tablespoons butter
4 cups finely chopped head lettuce
2 tablespoons flour
1 cup half-and-half (half milk, half cream)
2 cups chicken broth (canned or freshly made)
  About ½ teaspoon salt
2 tablespoons chopped chives, fresh, frozen, or
  freeze-dried
1 tablespoon Roquefort cheese, mashed
½ cup heavy cream

Melt butter in a wide frying pan. Add lettuce and cook quickly, stirring, until limp. (If you like smooth soups, whirl cooked lettuce in a blender or rub through a wire strainer.) Blend in flour and gradually add half-and-half, chicken broth, and salt. Simmer, stirring, for 4 or 5 minutes. Add chives and pour into heat-proof soup bowls. Combine Roquefort cheese and heavy cream; whip cream softly and spoon mixture equally onto each bowl of soup. Broil about 6 inches from heat until cream is lightly browned (1 to 2 minutes). Makes 4 to 6 servings.

Cream of Mushroom Soup

You can make smooth cream of mushroom soup ahead and refrigerate it, if you wish. Heat to just below boiling and serve.

5 cups sliced mushrooms
¼ medium-sized onion, sliced
3 tablespoons butter or margarine
1 tablespoon flour
½ teaspoon salt
½ teaspoon thyme
  Dash pepper
2 teaspoons tomato paste
1 tablespoon lemon juice
4 cups milk or half-and-half (half milk,
  half cream)

Sauté mushrooms and onion in butter or margarine until vegetables are just tender. Blend in flour, salt, thyme, and pepper; when bubbling, stir and cook about 1 minute. Then blend in tomato paste, lemon juice, and 1 cup of the milk or half-and-half. Pour mixture, a portion at a time, into blender container and add the remaining 3 cups milk or half-and-half. Whirl until smooth. If you want an exceptionally smooth soup, force liquid through a fine wire strainer into a pan. Reheat to serve, but do not boil. Makes about 5 cups soup.

Chilled Avocado Soup

Puréed avocado makes this soup a velvety smooth, pastel green color.

1 large avocado, peeled and pitted
½ cup half-and-half (half milk, half cream)
1½ cups chicken broth (freshly made, canned, or
  made from chicken stock concentrate)
  Salt
  Garlic salt
  Chopped chives
  Commercial sour cream (optional)
  Paprika (optional)

Place avocado pieces in a blender container and blend until smooth. Add half-and-half and chicken broth, and blend a few seconds. Then season to taste with salt and garlic salt; chill. Garnish with chopped chives or, if you wish, top each serving with a spoonful of sour cream and sprinkle lightly with paprika. Makes 6 servings.

Chilled Sour Cream Cucumber Soup

Thin custard sauce is the base for the following chilled soup. You continue to enrich it by folding in sour cream, wine, and cucumbers.

2 cups milk
3 eggs, beaten
1 cup commercial sour cream
1 cup chicken broth (canned or freshly made)
½ cup dry white wine
1½ cups finely chopped, peeled cucumber
2 tablespoons finely chopped green onion
1 tablespoon finely chopped pimiento
About 1 teaspoon salt
¼ teaspoon dill weed
Paper thin slices unpeeled cucumber
Shredded or grated Parmesan cheese or paprika

Heat milk over direct heat in top part of double boiler. Gradually stir in beaten eggs. Place over hot water and cook, stirring, until mixture coats a metal spoon in a velvety, opaque layer. Remove from heat and cool. Add some of the custard to the sour cream; then return sour cream to custard. Stir in broth, wine, cucumber, green onion, pimiento, salt, and dill. Chill thoroughly. Garnish each bowlful with cucumber slices topped with cheese or paprika. Makes about 1½ quarts.

Tropical Soup

The simplicity of tropical soup makes it an entertaining favorite.

1 can (10¾ oz.) condensed cream of chicken soup
1 can (10¾ oz.) condensed cream of celery soup
¾ cup half-and-half (half milk, half cream)
2 cups milk
½ teaspoon salt
Dash white pepper
1 medium-sized avocado, peeled and diced
½ cup sliced pitted ripe or green ripe olives

Blend together in a pan the chicken soup, celery soup, half-and-half, milk, salt, and white pepper. Heat until simmering; stir in avocado and olives and serve. Makes 8 servings.

Black Bean Soup

Garnishes of sliced lemon and chopped hard-cooked egg add to the distinctive flavor of smooth black bean soup.

1 can (10½ oz.) condensed black bean soup
1 can (10½ oz.) condensed beef consommé
1 tablespoon sherry, Madeira, or lemon juice
1 tablespoon rum (optional)
1 lemon, thinly sliced
3 hard-cooked eggs
Minced parsley

Put in the blender the black bean soup, consommé, sherry, and rum; blend until smooth. Pour into a pan and heat, but do not boil. Spoon into bowls; float a lemon slice on top of each serving; sprinkle with sieved hard-cooked egg yolks, chopped egg whites, and parsley. Makes 4 to 6 servings. (If you double the recipe to serve 8, you might serve the soup from a tureen and pass a tray of the garnishes. Arrange the sieved yolks in the center of the tray; surround with the chopped egg whites, chopped parsley, and sliced lemon.)

Pretzel-topped cream of broccoli soup is presented in individual mugs to sip as a dinner appetizer. Whirled smooth in an electric blender, the soup can be made ahead and refrigerated until serving time.

WORKS WITH CELERY + OTHER VEGS   I USUALLY DO NOT PUREE

Cream of Broccoli Soup

Small pretzels garnish creamy broccoli soup.

1 C 1 can (14 oz.) or about 1¾ cups freshly made
   chicken broth

10 oz. 2 packages (10 oz. each) frozen chopped broccoli

   1 small bay leaf

2 T ¼ cup butter or margarine

2 T ¼ cup flour

   ¼ teaspoon salt

   Dash pepper

1 C 2 cups milk

   · ADD THYME

Pour the chicken broth over the broccoli in a 3-quart pan and add bay leaf. Bring to a boil and simmer gently about 5 minutes, or until broccoli is tender. Meanwhile, melt butter in a frying pan and stir in flour, salt, and pepper; cook about 1 minute, stirring. Gradually add the milk, stirring to make a smooth sauce. Remove from heat.

Remove bay leaf from broccoli mixture and pour broccoli and liquid into blender container, a portion at a time; whirl until smooth. Force mixture through a fine wire strainer back into the pan; stir in the milk sauce. Heat to simmering and serve. Makes about 6 cups.

Green Pea Cream Soup

This quick soup requires a package of frozen peas, milk, and an electric blender.

　1 package (10 oz.) frozen peas
　1 cup boiling water
　1 bay leaf
　¼ teaspoon thyme
　1 cup undiluted evaporated milk, or 1 cup
　　　whole milk
　½ teaspoon salt
　　Butter

Place frozen peas in boiling water seasoned with bay leaf and thyme; cook for 4 minutes after it returns to boil. Remove bay leaf. Pour peas with liquid into an electric blender; whirl until smooth. Return to pan and blend in milk and salt. Reheat to serve. Garnish servings with dots of butter. Makes 4 to 6 servings.

Minted Cream of Pea Soup

Minted cream of pea soup makes the most of the special affinity of mint and peas. Carry the coolness of green further by serving it with bread rounds spread with mayonnaise, chopped parsley, green peppers, and capers.

　1 can (10½ oz.) condensed green pea soup
　2 soup cans milk
　3 tablespoons finely chopped fresh mint
　1 teaspoon sugar
　2 teaspoons finely chopped chives
　⅛ teaspoon liquid hot-pepper seasoning
　½ cup half-and-half (half cream, half milk)
　　Commercial sour cream
　　Tiny mint sprigs for garnish

In a large pan, blend condensed soup, milk, chopped mint, sugar, chives, and liquid hot-pepper seasoning. Heat to simmering; cool. Stir in half-and-half; chill. Serve in bowls and garnish with spoonfuls of sour cream and tiny mint sprigs. Makes 4 servings.

Caldo Largo (Long Soup)

You add "heat" to this soup in the form of liquid hot-pepper seasoning.

　2 tablespoons salad oil
　2 medium-sized ripe tomatoes, peeled, seeded,
　　　and diced
　2 medium-sized green peppers, seeded and cut
　　　in thin strips
　1½ cups chicken broth (canned or freshly made)
　1 can (14½ oz.) evaporated milk
　　Salt
　　Liquid hot-pepper seasoning
　¼ pound jack cheese, diced

Heat oil in a wide pan; add tomatoes and peppers and cook until peppers are limp. Add broth and simmer slowly for about 10 minutes. Stir in milk; add salt and liquid hot-pepper seasoning to taste. Mix in the cheese and ladle immediately into soup bowls. Makes 4 to 6 servings.

Curried Cream of Corn Soup

Garnish each mug of curried cream of corn soup with a dash of paprika, a sprinkling of chopped parsley, or a little sour cream. Small pretzels, crackers, or croutons are also suitable garnishes.

　4 cups corn, fresh or frozen and thawed
　¼ medium-sized onion, sliced
　2 tablespoons butter or margarine
　2 tablespoons flour
　¾ teaspoon curry powder
　¼ teaspoon salt
　　Dash pepper
　2 cups chicken broth (canned or freshly made)
　2 cups milk

Sauté the corn and onion in the butter or margarine until corn is just tender, about 2 minutes. Stir in the flour, curry powder, salt, and pepper. Cook over medium heat, stirring, about 1 minute. Gradually stir in chicken broth, stirring until bubbling and slightly thickened. Pour mixture, a portion at a time, into blender container and add milk; whirl until smooth. Force soup through a fine wire strainer into a pan. To serve, heat to just under the boiling point. Makes about 5 cups.

Chilled Vegetable Soup

One delicious variation of vichyssoise combines potatoes with fresh green peas, curry powder, and celery salt.

> 1 cup coarsely diced raw potatoes
> 1 cup fresh or frozen green peas
> ¼ cup sliced green onions
> 1½ cups chicken broth (canned or freshly made)
> ⅛ teaspoon celery salt
> ⅛ teaspoon curry powder
> 1 cup heavy cream
>   Paprika (optional)
>   Chopped green onion tops or chopped chives
>   (optional)

Add the potatoes, peas, and green onions to the chicken broth in a pan. Bring to a boil; reduce heat, cover, and simmer until the vegetables are just tender, about 10 minutes. Pour vegetable mixture into blender and blend until smooth, or rub through a fine strainer. Mix in the celery salt, curry powder, and cream. Chill very thoroughly before serving. Serve in bouillon cups with a sprinkling of paprika and either chopped green onion tops or chopped chives. Makes about 4 servings.

Vichyssoise

A long-time favorite of the gourmet, chilled vichyssoise is not at all difficult to put together.

> 4 leeks or 1 large bunch green onions, finely
>   chopped (use white part only)
> 1 large onion, thinly sliced
> ¼ cup (⅛ lb.) butter or margarine
> 1 quart chicken broth (canned or freshly made)
>   or strong chicken bouillon (6 bouillon cubes
>   to 4 cups boiling water)
> 3 large potatoes, peeled and thinly sliced
> 1 cup (½ pt.) heavy cream
>   About 1 cup milk
>   Salt and pepper
>   Chopped chives or green onion tops

Over low heat, cook chopped leeks or green onions and sliced onion in butter until soft, but not browned. Add chicken broth and potatoes and cook, covered, until potatoes are tender, about 20 minutes. Press through a fine wire strainer, or blend smooth in an electric blender. Pour in cream and milk and season to taste with salt and pepper. If too thick, thin with additional milk. Chill thoroughly. Serve cold with finely chopped chives or chopped green onion tops sprinkled over the top. Makes 8 servings.

Cream of Spinach Soup

Frozen spinach provides the garden-fresh flavor for hot creamy spinach soup.

> 1 package (10 oz.) frozen chopped spinach
> 1 cup boiling chicken broth (canned, freshly
>   made, or made with chicken stock base)
> 2 tablespoons minced fresh parsley
> 2 egg yolks
> ½ teaspoon salt
>   Dash pepper
> 1 cup undiluted evaporated milk, or 1 cup
>   whole milk
>   Lemon slices

Place spinach in boiling chicken broth; cook for 2 minutes after it returns to a boil. Add parsley and pour into blender; whirl until smooth. Drop egg yolks into whirling soup. Season with salt and pepper. Return to pan and stir in milk. Reheat to serve. Float a lemon slice on each serving. Makes 4 to 6 servings.

Fresh Tomato Soup

(see suggested menu opposite)

Fresh tomato soup is equally suitable as a picnic opener or as the first course of a dinner party. You can keep the soup hot in a vacuum bottle to transport to a picnic.

- 2 cups peeled, diced ripe tomatoes
- 3 tablespoons butter
- 2 tablespoons flour
- 1 teaspoon salt
- Dash pepper
- ¼ teaspoon soda
- 1 cup half-and-half (half milk, half cream)
- ½ cup dry white wine or chicken broth (canned or freshly made)

Simmer the tomatoes in butter for about 5 minutes; rub through a wire strainer or whirl smooth in a blender. Sprinkle in flour, salt, and pepper, blending. Bring to a boil; reduce heat and cook for 2 or 3 minutes, stirring constantly. Add soda and half-and-half; cook until slightly thickened. Stir in wine or chicken broth and heat to simmering. Makes 4 to 6 servings.

Iced Fresh Tomato Soup

The flavor secret of this clear, herb-piquant soup is to use fully ripe tomatoes. Toasted cheese canapés are especially good with it. For a different garnish, top each serving with salted whipped cream.

- 4 pounds ripe tomatoes
- ¼ teaspoon dried basil
- 2 tablespoons chopped onion
- 1 cup chicken broth (canned or freshly made)
- 2 teaspoons sugar
- ½ teaspoon salt
- ¼ teaspoon pepper
- 1 cup dry white wine
- Cooked shrimp for garnish

Remove ends from tomatoes and cut into eighths. Force tomatoes, basil, and onion through food mill or whirl in a blender and pour through a wire strainer. Add chicken broth, sugar, salt, pepper, and white wine; whip to blend. Chill thoroughly. Stir before serving. Float shrimp on top. Makes 6 to 8 servings.

Hot Senegalese

A coriander-cream topping distinguishes hot senegalese; applesauce and curry blend subtly in the background.

- 3 tablespoons butter
- ½ cup finely chopped celery
- ¼ cup finely chopped onion
- ½ teaspoon curry powder
- 2 tablespoons flour
- ¾ cup canned sweetened applesauce
- 2 cups chicken broth (canned or freshly made)
- 2 cups half-and-half (half milk, half cream)
- Salt
- ¾ cup heavy cream
- ⅛ teaspoon ground coriander

Melt butter and add celery and onion; cook until soft. Blend in curry powder and flour; gradually add applesauce, chicken broth, and half-and-half. Heat to simmering and cook gently, stirring, for 4 or 5 minutes. Season to taste with salt. Pour into heat-proof bowls. Softly whip the heavy cream and stir in coriander. Spoon equal portions of cream onto each bowl. Broil about 6 inches below heat until cream browns (1 or 2 minutes). Makes 4 to 6 servings.

 **Memorable Picnic**

Fresh Tomato Soup
(see recipe opposite)
Wheat Crackers
Potato Salad Caesar
Open-Faced Sandwiches
Chocolate Cream Cups
Chocolate Refrigerator Cookies

With no more effort than you usually expend getting an ordinary picnic together, you can prepare this elegant outdoor meal. All the foods are simple to make and transport easily.

POTATO SALAD CAESAR

Beat together ½ cup salad oil, 1 teaspoon Worcestershire, 1 teaspoon salt, ⅛ teaspoon pepper, ⅛ teaspoon garlic powder, ¼ cup lemon juice, 1 egg, and ¼ cup minced green onion. Toss with 4 cups diced hot cooked potatoes; chill thoroughly. Spoon into a large, chilled salad bowl. Top with 2 quarts broken pieces crisp romaine. Cover with clear plastic wrap to carry to the picnic. (The cold bowl and salad will keep cool for several hours if kept in a shaded place.)

Carry along in individual containers: 2 cups croutons that have been tossed with 2 tablespoons melted butter and a pinch of garlic powder; ¼ cup grated Parmesan cheese and ¼ cup crumbled Roquefort cheese; 6 or 8 chopped anchovies; ½ cup sliced pitted ripe olives. To serve, combine all ingredients and toss. Makes 6 to 8 servings.

OPEN-FACED SANDWICHES

Spread slices of a favorite bread with butter; top each with luncheon meat, more butter, and cheese (butter holds it in place). Cut in fancy shapes. Arrange on a tray and wrap in foil. Chill and carry to the picnic.

CHOCOLATE CREAM CUPS

Prepare 1 package (4 oz.) chocolate or butterscotch pudding mix according to package directions using 1½ cups milk and ¼ cup sherry for the liquid. Add ⅛ teaspoon salt and 1 teaspoon instant coffee powder. Cover and chill. Fold in ½ cup heavy cream, whipped, and spoon into 6 or 8 individual serving cups (use crème pots or paper cups with lids) and cover. Carry to picnic in an insulated bag along with a covered bowl of spiced cream topping, made as follows: Whip ½ cup heavy cream; fold in 1 tablespoon sugar, ½ teaspoon instant coffee powder, and ⅛ teaspoon cinnamon. Serve on chocolate cream.

Swiss Chard Soup

In this recipe, first you cook the white center stalk of the Swiss chard; then you add the tender green leaves. In a wide, heavy pan, melt 2 tablespoons butter or margarine. Add chopped, heavy stems from 1 pound cleaned Swiss chard; cook covered, stirring occasionally, for 3 or 4 minutes. Stir in the chopped leaves and cook 3 or 4 minutes more.

Sprinkle with 2 tablespoons flour and stir until blended. Gradually blend in 1½ cups chicken broth (canned or freshly made) and ½ cup half-and-half (half milk, half cream) or milk; cook and stir until slightly thickened. Season to taste with salt and pepper. (If you prefer a smooth green soup, whirl mixture in a blender until it is the consistency desired, or rub through a fine wire strainer.) Makes 4 to 6 servings.

Plateau Soup (Yayla Corbasi)

Light and refreshing, plateau soup is named for its popularity in the plateau regions of Turkey. It is flavored with fresh mint and most often served hot, but it is also nice as a cold soup. You might serve it before an entrée of lamb or grilled meat.

1 can (10½ oz.) condensed beef bouillon, diluted with equal amount of water
2 tablespoons rice
2 tablespoons melted butter
1 tablespoon flour
4 tablespoons yogurt
1 egg yolk, slightly beaten
½ cup water
¼ teaspoon salt
1½ teaspoons finely chopped fresh mint

Bring diluted bouillon to a boil; add rice and cook until the rice is tender. In a separate pan, combine 1 tablespoon of the butter with the flour; stir in yogurt, egg yolk, water, and salt. Spoon about 3 tablespoons of the hot bouillon mixture into the yogurt mixture and stir to blend; combine with the hot bouillon. Remove from heat. Add mint to remaining butter and add to soup before serving. Makes 4 servings.

Yokohama Cream of Clam

Broiler-browned whipped cream tops a tasty blend of clam juice, cream, and wine.

2 tablespoons butter
2 tablespoons finely chopped shallots or green onions (white part only)
2 tablespoons flour
2 bottles (7 oz. each) clam juice
1 cup chicken broth (canned or freshly made)
1 cup half-and-half (half milk, half cream)
  Salt
¼ to ½ cup dry white wine
¾ cup heavy cream

Melt the butter in a saucepan. Add the shallots or green onions and cook until soft. Stir in flour

and gradually blend in clam juice, chicken broth, and half-and-half. Salt to taste, if needed. Cook, stirring, at a gentle boil for about 5 minutes. Blend in ¼ to ½ cup white wine, according to taste. Pour into heat-proof soup bowls. Softly whip the cream and spoon equal portions onto each bowl. Broil about 6 inches from heat until cream browns (1 or 2 minutes). Makes 4 to 6 servings.

Oyster Soup Deluxe

Smooth green purée of spinach is artfully seasoned with oysters. Broiled Hollandaise cream forms the soup topping.

1 can (8 oz.) oysters, undrained
1 package (10 oz.) frozen chopped spinach, thawed
3 tablespoons chopped onion
2 cups half-and-half (half milk, half cream)
1 teaspoon Worcestershire
  About 2 tablespoons lemon juice
  Salt
¼ cup heavy cream
¼ cup Hollandaise sauce (canned or freshly made)

Whirl oysters, spinach, and onion in a blender until smooth or force through a fine wire strainer. Combine in a pan with the half-and-half, Worcestershire, lemon juice to taste, and salt to season. Heat soup to simmering and cook gently for about 5 minutes. Pour into heat-proof soup bowls. Softly whip the cream and fold in Hollandaise sauce. Spoon equal portions onto each bowl of soup. Broil about 6 inches below heat until topping browns— 1 or 2 minutes. (If you would like whole oysters in the soup, drain another can—8 oz.—oysters and add the shellfish to the soup before adding the topping.) Makes 4 to 6 servings.

Pacific Oyster Bisque

Make Pacific oyster bisque shortly before it is to be served; the consistency is affected if it stands.

2 quarts milk
1 bay leaf
4 celery tops, washed
4 sprigs parsley
1 medium-sized onion, chopped
½ cup (¼ lb.) butter or margarine
3 slices whole lemon
2 teaspoons salt
⅛ teaspoon pepper
2 containers (12 oz. each) Pacific oysters
4 egg yolks

Using a large double boiler or a pan set over boiling water; scald milk with the bay, celery, and parsley. Meanwhile sauté the onion in butter until soft. Add the lemon slices, salt, pepper, and oysters, including their liquor; cover, and cook until edges of oysters begin to curl, about 10 minutes. Discard lemon slices.

Remove about half the oysters to a cutting board, chop, and reserve. Turn remaining oyster-onion mixture into blender container; whirl until smooth; add egg yolks and whirl a few seconds more. Remove celery, bay, and parsley from the milk and add the blended oyster mixture; stir over slowly simmering water until slightly thickened. Stir in chopped oysters. Reduce heat, cover, and keep warm over hot (not boiling) water. Makes about 12 servings.

This first-course oyster bisque is served buffet style in the family room (the patio is also a good place) with tiny corn muffins, relishes in a bowl of freshly crushed ice, and sherry.

Fruit Soups

Strawberry-Loganberry Soup

Because of their delicate structure, strawberries break up easily when cooked; here they are forced through a wire strainer so the soup will have a clear ruby color without bits of seeds and pulp. Try serving strawberry-loganberry soup warm for breakfast, cold for lunch, or chilled with a dollop of whipped cream as a dessert.

> 2 cups water
> 3 cups sliced or crushed strawberries
>   Sugar to taste (¼ to ½ cup)
> 2 tablespoons cornstarch
> 1½ tablespoons lemon juice
>   ½ cup canned loganberry juice
>   1 cup whole strawberries, hulled

Heat water in a pan; add the sliced strawberries and sugar to taste; bring to a boil. Whirl berry mixture in a blender and pour through a wire strainer (or force berry mixture through a wire strainer and discard pulp). Blend cornstarch with a small amount of the liquid; combine with the rest of berry mixture and bring to a boil quickly, stirring to prevent lumping. Stir in lemon juice and loganberry juice. Serve hot or cold (chill, covered) with whole strawberries floating in the soup. Makes 4 to 5 servings.

Peach and Plum Soup

When combined, peaches and plums are exceptionally flavorful. The mild tartness of peach and plum soup suits it to brunch; or, topped with whipped cream and slivered almonds, it makes a delicious dessert.

> 2 cups water
> 1 cup peeled peach slices
> 1 cup plum slices (such as Santa Rosas)
>   Sugar to taste (¼ to ½ cup)
> 2 tablespoons cornstarch
> 1 tablespoon lemon juice
>   Additional peach or plum slices

In a saucepan, bring water to a boil and simmer fruit slices 15 to 20 minutes or until soft. Whirl in a blender and pour through a wire strainer (or force mixture through a wire strainer); discard pulp. Add sugar to taste. Blend cornstarch with a small amount of juice; add to fruit mixture and quickly bring to a boil, stirring to prevent lumping. Stir in lemon juice. Chill, covered, and serve with slices of fresh fruit in each serving as garnish. Makes 4 to 5 servings.

Peach Soup

Offer peach soup at lunch time on a hot summer day. Follow the directions for peach and plum soup on this page, with these variations: Omit plums and use a total of 2 cups peach slices. Add 1 teaspoon almond extract and garnish with slivered almonds or peach slices. Makes 4 to 5 servings.

Apricot Citrus

Because of its citrus liveliness, this soup is good for breakfast, brunch, or as a first course. Follow the directions for peach and plum soup on this page, but use a total of 2 cups of apricots in place of the peaches and plums. (If you prefer, substitute 2 cans—12 oz. each—apricot nectar for the fruit and water.) After thickening the soup, stir in the lemon juice, 3 tablespoons lime juice, and ½ cup orange juice. Garnish with thin slices of lime. Makes 4 to 5 servings.

Cherry Soup

Fruit soup for breakfast is easy because you make it the night before to allow it to chill. Zwieback toast complements it nicely.

Follow the directions for peach and plum soup on page 52, but use a total of 3 cups sweet cherries, pitted, instead of the peaches and plums. Add a 3 to 4-inch cinnamon stick to the simmering fruit; then discard. Increase the lemon juice to 1½ tablespoons. Float an additional 1 cup pitted sweet cherries in the soup. Makes 4 to 5 servings.

Spiced Rhubarb Soup

Delicate pink in color, spiced rhubarb soup makes a refreshing opening to a warm weather luncheon. Choose a light, flower-scented wine, such as Chenin Blanc or Gewürztraminer, to add to the soup.

4 cups (about 1¼ pounds) diced rhubarb
4 cups (1 quart) water
1 cup sugar
1 teaspoon grated orange peel
3-inch stick cinnamon
2 tablespoons arrowroot starch or cornstarch
½ cup water
½ teaspoon vanilla
Few drops red food coloring (optional)
About ½ cup dry white wine
Whole cloves
Thin orange slices

Place rhubarb in a 3-quart pan with water, sugar, orange peel, and cinnamon. Bring to a boil, reduce heat, and simmer for about 20 minutes. Blend arrowroot with the ½ cup water and stir the mixture into the rhubarb. Bring to a boil, then remove from heat. Add vanilla and red food coloring, if needed, to tint a delicate pink; cool. Place in a glass or earthenware bowl, and refrigerate, covered, until thoroughly chilled. Add about 1 tablespoon of the wine to each serving. Serve garnished with clove-studded orange slices. Makes 6 to 8 servings.

Lemon Meringue Soup

A filling, frothy cross between lemon meringue pie and lemonade, serve lemon meringue soup as a dessert or afternoon snack.

4 tablespoons cornstarch
4 cups water
Peel of 2 lemons (pared with vegetable peeler)
Juice of 2 lemons
¾ cup sugar
1 tablespoon dry white wine (optional)
2 egg yolks
4 egg whites
Lemon or lime slices

Blend cornstarch with a small amount of the water. Combine with rest of water, lemon peel, lemon juice, ¼ cup of the sugar, and wine. Bring to a boil and cook, stirring, until slightly thickened and clear. Remove from heat; add a little of the hot mixture to egg yolks and then add yolks to the soup, beating constantly. Remove peel if desired. Chill soup thoroughly, covered. Beat egg whites until stiff; add ½ cup sugar, a little at a time. Beat until whites form stiff, glossy peaks. Set aside a small amount of the meringue for garnish and whip the cold soup into the remaining meringue. Serve immediately with dollops of meringue topped with a lemon or lime slice in each bowl. Makes 6 to 8 servings.

LIGHT BUT SATISFYING SOUPS

For lunch and supper

Each of the satisfying, rather homey soups in this chapter can form the nucleus for a fine light menu with the proper support from such additional foods as sandwiches, salads, cheeses, cold meats, sausages, and breads. Most of these soups derive their body and flavor from one or more vegetables and just enough meat, fish, or cheese (if any at all) to season well. Thus they have a nice built-in flexibility; you can dress them up or down, and make the meal more or less substantial, as you like.

Consider these possibilities: Chilled cucumber soup with lean roast beef, ideal for a bridge luncheon and perfect for dieters; cheese soup with condiments, green salad, and peach shortcake in peach season; cream of spinach soup with smoked salmon, cream cheese, and bagels for a late supper after a show. Chilled green garden soup with liver paté sandwiches for a summer party lunch; or lentil soup with broiled garlic sausages, dark bread, and butter for big eaters.

Shortcut cookery is abundantly used in these recipes. Many of the soups start with a canned or packaged ingredient and require just one or two personal touches to give them a fresh aspect. Some of the soups benefit by reheating and can be made well ahead; others, like pea soups with cheese, are so quick to make that there is no advantage in starting too soon. The soups that begin from scratch, in the old-fashioned sense, really don't demand much preparation either. The hours that they cook can take no more attention than an occasional stir, such as for the Bellingham split pea soup. A similar technique is used for the brisket and asparagus soup, where you first cook the meat to get the broth to make the soup.

Iced fruit soup for lunch: Add a big spoonful of sour cream to this clear borsch made with beets, broth, and Bing cherries. Recipe on page 59.

Vegetable Soups

Brisket and Asparagus Soup

Delicately flavored broth extracted from the cooking of fresh beef brisket is an ideal base for soup flavored with asparagus. You can make spinach or squash soup with the brisket stock by making the substitutions that follow. The natural soup accompaniment is the brisket, sliced and served cold or heated in a little butter.

        3 pounds fresh beef brisket
        4 cups water
        2 medium-sized onions, cut in pieces
        2 medium-sized carrots, cut in pieces
        4 sprigs parsley
        1 bay leaf
        ½ teaspoon marjoram
        8 whole black peppers
    1½ teaspoons salt
        2 cups thinly sliced asparagus

Trim and discard most of the fat from brisket. Place brisket in a deep pan; add water, onions, carrots, parsley, bay leaf, marjoram, whole black peppers, and salt. Bring to a boil; reduce heat. Cover and simmer about 3½ hours or until brisket is tender when pierced. Remove brisket and chill, covered, for any use desired; strain stock and chill. When stock is cold, skim off fat. Whirl asparagus in a blender with a small amount of stock until smooth (or cook asparagus until just tender in a small amount of the stock; then force through a wire strainer). Combine stock with asparagus mixture. Bring to boiling and simmer 5 minutes. Makes 6 to 8 servings.

BRISKET AND SQUASH SOUP:

Follow the directions above for brisket and asparagus soup, but omit the asparagus and add 2 cups thinly sliced, uncooked crookneck squash to stock. (Do not whirl squash in a blender.) Bring to a boil and cook until the squash is tender, about 5 minutes.

BRISKET AND SPINACH SOUP:

Follow the directions given left for brisket and asparagus soup, but use 2 cups cooked spinach instead of the asparagus.

Asparagus Cream Soup

Hot creamy purée of asparagus and a favorite sandwich make a quick lunch or supper.

        1 package (10 oz.) frozen cut asparagus
        ½ cup boiling chicken broth (canned, freshly
                made, made with water and bouillon cube
                or 1½ teaspoons chicken stock base)
        2 egg yolks
    1¼ cups milk
        ½ teaspoon salt
        ¼ teaspoon pepper
        2 drops of liquid hot-pepper seasoning
                Minced parsley
                Paprika

Place frozen asparagus in boiling chicken stock; cook, uncovered, for 8 minutes after it returns to a boil. Whirl asparagus and liquid in an electric blender until smooth (or force through a fine wire strainer); drop egg yolks into blending mixture. Return to pan and stir in whole milk, salt, pepper, and liquid hot-pepper seasoning. Reheat just before serving, but do not boil. Top each serving with the minced parsley and the paprika. Makes 4 to 6 servings.

Georgian Beet Soup

Canned and dry ingredients create the sweet-sour borsch-like base for this soup; the whipped cream topping is broiled.

1 envelope (1½ to 1¾ oz.) dry onion soup mix
  Water
1 can (1 lb.) pickled sliced beets and liquid
1 can (6 oz.) Vienna sausages, drained and thinly sliced
1 cup commercial sour cream
½ cup heavy cream
¼ cup chopped chives (fresh, frozen, freeze-dried)

Prepare the onion soup mix according to directions on the package, decreasing the water by 1 cup. Add the beets, beet liquid, and sliced Vienna sausages. Heat together for 2 or 3 minutes. Remove from heat and blend some of liquid thoroughly with the sour cream; then return all to pan. Pour into heat-proof bowls. Softly whip the cream and fold in the chives; spoon onto each bowl of soup. Broil about 6 inches below heat until cream browns (1 or 2 minutes). Makes 4 to 6 servings.

Spoon flavored whipped cream onto Georgian beet soup and place under broiler until surface of cream is bubbling brown. Dried onion soup mix forms the base of the soup, with Vienna sausages and beets added.

Lentil Soup

Lentils seasoned by a variety of vegetables and a little bacon make a filling winter soup.

 2 cups lentils
 2 quarts water
 2 slices uncooked bacon, cut in pieces
 1 medium-sized onion, sliced
 ¼ cup chopped carrots
 ½ cup chopped celery
 3 tablespoons chopped parsley
 1 clove garlic, minced or mashed (or 1 teaspoon garlic juice)
 2 teaspoons salt
 ¼ teaspoon pepper
 ½ teaspoon oregano
 1 can (1 lb.) solid pack tomatoes
 2 tablespoons wine vinegar

Wash the lentils and place them in a pan with the water, bacon, onion, carrots, celery, parsley, garlic, salt, pepper, and oregano. Cover pan and simmer for 1½ hours. Add the tomatoes and break them up with a spoon; add the vinegar and simmer 30 minutes longer. Taste, and add more salt if needed. Makes about 10 servings.

Corn and Tomato Chowder

Swimming with cheese, this colorful vegetable chowder makes a nourishing schoolday lunch. With it, you might serve old-fashioned crisp water crackers.

 2 cups corn (freshly cooked or canned)
 1 cup canned tomatoes
 1 cup diced celery
 3 cups water
 1 teaspoon salt
 2 tablespoons butter
 3 tablespoons flour
 1½ cups milk
 ½ cup shredded Cheddar cheese
 1 green pepper, finely chopped
 Salt and pepper to taste

In a medium-sized pan combine corn, tomatoes, celery, water, and salt. Bring to a boil and simmer 30 minutes. Meanwhile, in a small pan, melt butter and blend in flour and then milk. Cook, stirring, until thickened. Combine with vegetables. Stir in cheese, green pepper, and season with salt and pepper. Makes 6 to 8 servings.

Mayan Bean Soup

Similar to the hearty bean soup served in restaurants in Yucatan, Mexico, this version is easy to make. Packaged corn chips are a good accompaniment, but if you want to emphasize the soup's Mexican character, serve it with tacos, tostadas, or fried tortillas.

 1 can (11½ oz.) condensed bean with bacon soup
 1 soup can water
 ½ cup cooked or canned whole kernel corn
 ½ of a whole canned pimiento
   Dash garlic powder, or ½ small clove garlic, minced or mashed
 1 tablespoon prepared taco sauce, or about ½ teaspoon salsa picante (Mexican hot sauce), or dash liquid hot-pepper seasoning

In a pan combine the soup with the water and bring to simmering. As the soup heats, stir in the cooked or canned corn.

With kitchen scissors or a knife, cut the pimiento into pieces about the size of corn kernels; stir pimiento into the soup along with the garlic and the taco sauce. Bring to a boil and simmer for 5 minutes. Makes 2 generous servings as a main dish, or 4 servings as a first course.

Cherry Borsch *(see suggested menu below)*

Nest servings of this ruby red borsch in crushed ice; the flavor is typically sweet-sour, and the cherries are a surprising, but well suited ingredient.

2 cans (14 oz. each) beef broth
2 to 3-inch stick cinnamon
1 can (1 lb.) pickled beets, well drained with
    liquid reserved, chopped
2 tablespoons brown sugar
  About 1 pound fresh Bing cherries, washed,
    stemmed, pitted
  Lemon juice (optional)
  Commercial sour cream

Bring to a boil the beef broth and cinnamon stick. Add the chopped beets, beet liquid, and brown sugar. Heat until boiling again; then add the cherries and quickly return to boil. Remove cinnamon stick if spice flavor is strong enough to taste, or leave it in if the flavor is not yet noticeable. Cover soup and chill thoroughly. Add a little lemon juice if you want a more tart flavor. Ladle the soup into individual bowls and add a large spoonful of sour cream to each portion. Makes 4 or 5 servings.

Fruit Soup Lunch

Cherry Borsch *(see recipe above)*
Hot Corned Beef on Dark Rye Bread
Mustard
Cold Hard-Cooked Eggs   Dill Pickles
Cheesecake

This luncheon menu has a decided Russian character with a fresh cherry borsch. The corned beef sandwiches are filled with a multitude of thin meat slices heated in butter.

Make the soup in the morning to allow ample time for it to chill thoroughly. Serve the hard-cooked eggs in their shells, or shell them, as you prefer. Cheesecake can come from the freezer (homemade or purchased), or from the bakery.

HOT CORNED BEEF ON DARK RYE BREAD

Allow ¼ pound very thinly sliced corned beef for each sandwich and 1 sandwich per person. Heat the slices of corned beef over high heat in a wide frying pan lightly coated with butter; lay each slice flat in the pan; then push it to one side almost immediately, making room for another piece. Repeat until all the meat is in the pan and heated. Place equal portions of the meat between slices of dark rye bread to make each sandwich.

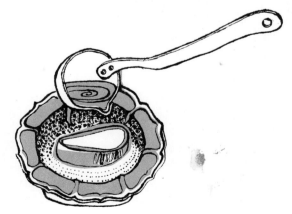

Irish Cabbage Soup

(see suggested menu below)

Potatoes provide a substantial background in this cabbage soup.

   2 medium-sized potatoes, peeled and diced
   1 medium-sized onion, chopped
   2 carrots, chopped
   1 medium-sized cabbage, shredded
   3 cups boiling water
   ½ teaspoon thyme
   1 bay leaf
1½ teaspoons salt
   ½ teaspoon pepper
   1 cup half-and-half (half milk, half cream)

Add the potatoes, onion, carrots, and cabbage to the boiling water. (Parboil the cabbage separately for about 10 minutes if you prefer a milder cabbage flavor.) Add thyme, bay leaf, salt, and pepper. Bring soup to a boil and simmer about 45 minutes, or until vegetables are tender but not mushy. Then add the half-and-half and heat (do not boil). Serve hot. Makes 6 servings.

Mushroom Soup Paprika

Sour cream blended with mushroom broth gives this soup a wonderful tang. You can prepare the soup ahead of time and reheat for the final steps.

½ pound mushrooms
   1 tablespoon butter or margarine
   1 teaspoon paprika
   1 tablespoon flour
   2 tablespoons finely chopped parsley
   4 cups beef broth (canned, freshly made, or made
      with beef stock concentrate)
   1 egg yolk
½ pint (1 cup) commercial sour cream

Slice mushrooms thinly into a pan. Sauté in butter along with paprika for 5 minutes, or until golden brown. Sprinkle mushrooms with flour and parsley. Gradually stir in beef broth and simmer slowly 30 minutes. Beat egg yolk slightly; blend with sour cream, and pour into a soup tureen. Gradually stir the hot soup into the tureen. Ladle into soup bowls. Makes 6 servings.

 An Irish Lunch

Irish Cabbage Soup *(see recipe above)*
Ham, Swiss Cheese, and Onion Sandwiches
Fresh Fruit
Milk or Coffee

The soup for this hearty lunch may be prepared early in the day; just add the half-and-half (half milk, half cream) and heat before serving. You can make the sandwiches ahead and wrap in plastic film, or pass a tray of sandwich fixings and let each person make his own. The dessert of fresh apples, pears, and grapes forms an attractive centerpiece.

HAM, SWISS CHEESE, AND ONION SANDWICHES

The typical Irish ham sandwich is made with thick slices of boiled or baked ham. Spread slices of bread, preferably a firm-textured white bread, with hot mustard. Add slices of ham, Swiss cheese, and red onion.

Hearty Irish cabbage soup is served for lunch with sandwiches of ham, cheese, onion, and mustard. You can prepare the soup early in the day; just add the half-and-half and heat before serving.

Mushroom-Potato Soup

½ *pound fresh mushrooms*
3 *tablespoons butter or margarine*
1 *small onion, finely chopped*
3 *tablespoons flour*
5 *cups boiling water*
2 *cups cubed raw potato*
1½ *teaspoons salt*
⅛ *teaspoon pepper*
2 *teaspoons Worcestershire*
2 *tablespoons chopped parsley*
1 *tablespoon lemon juice*
   Commercial sour cream
   Minced parsley

Remove stems from mushrooms and chop them. Slice the mushroom caps. Heat the butter in a heavy pan (at least 4-quart size). Add the chopped and sliced mushrooms and the onion; sauté, stirring, until mushrooms are lightly browned.

Stir in flour and continue cooking until flour has browned lightly. Gradually stir in water until blended. Add potatoes, salt, pepper, Worcestershire, parsley, and lemon juice. Cover pan and cook over medium low heat, stirring occasionally, until potatoes are tender, about 30 minutes. Serve in heated bowls; top each portion with a spoonful of sour cream and sprinkle on minced parsley. Makes 8 servings.

Pea Soup with Cheese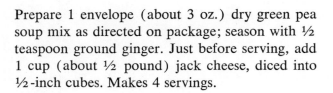

(see suggested menu below)

Prepare 1 envelope (about 3 oz.) dry green pea soup mix as directed on package; season with ½ teaspoon ground ginger. Just before serving, add 1 cup (about ½ pound) jack cheese, diced into ½-inch cubes. Makes 4 servings.

Bellingham Split Pea Soup

Cook a smoked beef tongue and use the broth to make Bellingham split pea soup. Serve the cold sliced tongue as an accompaniment.

2 cups dried split green peas
2 quarts liquor from boiling smoked tongue (or canned condensed beef consommé, diluted according to label directions)
1 stalk celery, sliced
1 large onion, chopped
1 large carrot, sliced
2 pounds fresh peas, shelled, or 1½ packages (10 oz. each) frozen peas
 Water
1 bay leaf
¼ teaspoon thyme
 Salt and pepper to taste
2 cups half-and-half (half milk, half cream)

 # Soup-and-Sandwich Lunch

Pea Soup with Cheese
(see recipe above)
Open-Faced Ham and Relish Sandwiches
Chilled Pears with Hot Chocolate Sauce

This lunch is designed to serve four, but you can easily double quantities to serve larger numbers. Place canned pear halves in the refrigerator several hours ahead to chill. While the soup simmers, make the sandwiches. Dice cheese into cubes; these are added to the pea soup just before serving so that they partially melt into it. Heat the chocolate sauce in the top of the double boiler and have ready to pour over the chilled pears for dessert.

OPEN-FACED HAM SANDWICHES

For each sandwich, butter 1 slice pumpernickel bread. Spread with 2 to 3 teaspoons sweet pickle relish; top with 2 thin slices Danish cooked ham, each rolled to form a cornucopia or tube. Garnish with lettuce, celery, and olives. Eat sandwiches with knife and fork.

CHILLED PEARS WITH HOT CHOCOLATE SAUCE

Chill drained canned Bartlett pear halves (1 or 2 per serving). Just before serving, spoon 1 or 2 tablespoons heated, canned chocolate sauce over each dessert. Top with toasted chopped almonds.

Wash split peas and put in a large kettle with the tongue liquor, celery, onion, and carrot; cover and simmer until tender, about 1½ to 2 hours.

Meanwhile, cook fresh peas, uncovered, in a small amount of water until just tender. Press both the soup and the cooked fresh peas through a strainer, or purée the peas in a blender and combine with the soup. Add the bay leaf, thyme, salt, and pepper, and simmer for 10 minutes longer to blend flavors. Add the cream; heat to simmering and serve. Makes 8 to 10 servings.

Viennese Potato Cream Soup

Viennese potato cream soup, hot or chilled, suits any season.

2 medium-sized potatoes, peeled and cut into
    ½-inch cubes
2 cups water
1 small onion, chopped, or 1 tablespoon instant
    minced onion
2 teaspoons chicken stock base
½ teaspoon salt
    Dash pepper
1 tablespoon flour
2 cups milk
½ teaspoon marjoram (optional)
    1 cup commercial sour cream
    Chopped fresh chives or freeze-dried chives

Add potatoes to the water with the onion, chicken stock base, salt, and pepper; cover and cook until the potatoes are tender (but not soft), 5 to 7 minutes. Meanwhile blend the flour with milk; gradually stir into the soup, and simmer, uncovered, for about 5 minutes. Season with marjoram, if desired. Reduce heat, add some of the hot soup to the sour cream, then stir back into soup; heat but do not boil.

To serve chilled, remove from heat before you add sour cream. Combine in the blender with the sour cream; whirl smooth. Chill thoroughly. Sprinkle each bowl with chopped chives. Makes about 6 servings.

Leek and Potato Soup

This soup was a forerunner of vichyssoise, but its function is quite different. It is served hot, in large bowls, and makes a fine meal when augmented with a green salad and crusty bread.

1 bunch leeks (usually 3 large ones, or 4 or 5
    smaller ones)
2 tablespoons butter
2 pounds potatoes, peeled and diced
2 quarts water or chicken broth (canned or
    freshly made)
½ cup half-and-half (half milk, half cream)
    Salt and pepper
    Minced parsley
    Crisp croutons

Wash the leeks very thoroughly and discard the tough part of the green tops. Cut in thin slices and again rinse, draining well. Cook in the butter until soft. Add diced potatoes, water or chicken broth, and simmer for 40 minutes. Add cream and salt and pepper to taste. Sprinkle with minced parsley and serve with crisp croutons. (This soup may be whirled in a blender to make a purée. If it becomes too thick, add milk, cream, or broth until you obtain the desired consistency.) Makes about 8 generous servings.

Cream of Spinach Soup

Nutmeg and thyme accent the fresh flavor in cream of spinach soup.

> 1 bunch (about ¾ pound) fresh spinach
> 2 tablespoons butter
> 2 cups milk or half-and-half (half milk, half cream)
> 2 tablespoons flour
> ⅛ teaspoon thyme
>   Dash nutmeg
> ½ teaspoon salt
>   Commercial sour cream
>   Croutons

Wash spinach well to remove all sand. Cut off root ends. Melt butter in a large pan, add the spinach, cover, and cook over high heat for 5 minutes or until spinach is limp. Pour into an electric blender and whirl until smooth, or press through wire strainer to make a purée. Mix the milk or cream with the flour and add to the spinach. Return spinach to pan; add the thyme, nutmeg, and salt. Cook over medium heat, stirring, until thickened. Serve **hot** with sour cream and croutons added to each portion. Makes 4 servings.

Beef Shank and Onion Soup

Succulent bits of marrow and tender portions of beef give body to this clear broth, permeated with the essence of onion.

> 2 slices (about 2 lbs.) center cut beef shank
> 4 cups water
> 2 medium-sized onions, sliced
> 1 medium-sized carrot, diced
> 3 sprigs parsley
> ¼ teaspoon whole allspice
> ⅛ teaspoon thyme
> ⅛ teaspoon rosemary
> ⅛ teaspoon marjoram
> ½ teaspoon basil
> 1 bay leaf
> 8 whole black peppers
> 1½ teaspoons salt

Pumpkin Soup

(see suggested menu opposite)

This is a peasant soup, filling and tasteful.

> 1 quart rich milk (or milk and part heavy cream)
> 1 medium-sized onion, sliced
> 4 whole cloves
> 4 sprigs parsley, bruised by pressing with the back of a spoon
> 1 clove garlic, pressed
> ¼ of a whole nutmeg, grated
> 1 bay leaf
> 1 tablespoon chicken stock concentrate (or 3 chicken bouillon cubes)
> 2 cups canned pumpkin
> 1 teaspoon salt
>   Freshly ground pepper
> 1 tablespoon lemon juice
>   Minced parsley
>   About 6 teaspoons butter

Scald the milk with the onion, cloves, parsley, garlic, nutmeg, bay leaf, and chicken stock concentrate. Add the pumpkin, salt, and pepper. Cook over hot water for 15 minutes; pour through a wire strainer and add lemon juice to soup. Serve with a sprinkle of minced parsley and about 1 teaspoon butter on top of each bowlful. Makes 6 servings.

Combine in a deep pan the beef shank, water, onions, carrot, parsley, allspice, thyme, rosemary, marjoram, basil, bay leaf, whole black peppers, and salt. Bring to a boil. Cover and simmer about 3 hours, or until meat is tender when pierced. Strain stock and chill; save meat and marrow; discard bones and fat. When stock is chilled, skim and discard fat. Cut meat and marrow in small pieces. Add pieces to the stock, heat and serve. Makes 6 to 8 servings.

Onion and Potato Soup

Creamy onion and potato soup has a sweet-sour flavor enhanced by a dry white wine, such as Chablis or sauterne. A blender hastens the puréeing of the vegetables.

3 medium-sized onions, chopped
2 tablespoons butter or margarine
2½ cups beef broth or bouillon (canned or freshly made)
¼ teaspoon celery flakes
1 medium-sized potato, thinly sliced
½ cup dry white wine
1½ teaspoons white wine vinegar
1 tablespoon finely chopped parsley
½ cup half-and-half (half milk, half cream)
Salt and pepper

Sauté onions in butter until soft and golden. Add beef broth, celery flakes, and potato. Cover and simmer about 30 minutes or until potato is very tender. Whirl in a blender until puréed, or press through a wire strainer or food mill; add wine and vinegar. Bring the mixture to a boil, reduce heat, and simmer about 5 minutes. Add parsley, cream, and salt and pepper to taste. Reheat, but do not allow to boil. Makes 4 servings, about 1 cup each.

After-Thanksgiving Lunch

Pumpkin Soup (Potage Potirons)
(see recipe opposite)
Turkey and Cress Sandwiches
Fried Apple Slices

This after-the-holiday meal uses the leftover canned pumpkin in a soup, and the turkey in a refreshing sandwich with watercress. You can, of course, serve the meal any time you have cold roast turkey.

TURKEY AND CRESS SANDWICHES

Combine 2 cups chopped cooked turkey meat with 2 cups watercress leaves (no stems) and ¾ cup mayonnaise. Season with salt to taste and add 2 chopped green onions or ¼ cup minced celery. Spread on toasted buttered bread. Makes enough filling to generously cover 6 to 8 toast slices.

Add this garnish if you wish: Peel and core 3 large apples and slice very thin. Sauté quickly in ¼ cup butter. When partly browned, sprinkle with 2 tablespoons sugar and continue cooking until tender. Cut toasted sandwiches in half; put on individual plates and place a spoonful of apple slices on each sandwich. Makes 6 to 8 servings.

Spiced Tomato Soup *(see suggested menu below)*

Combine in a saucepan 2 cups tomato juice, 2 cups beef broth (canned or freshly made), 6 whole black peppers, 3 cloves, ½ bay leaf, and 2 tablespoons lemon juice. Heat to boiling and simmer slowly for 10 minutes. Pour soup through a wire strainer; discard residue. Serve in bowls or cups, garnished individually with a slice of lemon. Makes 4 servings.

Low-Calorie Luncheon

Spiced Tomato Soup
(see recipe above)
Open-Faced Tongue Sandwiches
Pineapple-Buttermilk Sherbet

Here is a lunch that will fit easily into a busy schedule; perhaps you'll find occasion for such a meal preceding an afternoon of bridge or shopping.

Make the sandwiches with thinly sliced, canned pork tongue; arrange the meat on slim pieces of toasted whole wheat bread, which have been spread lightly with dark mustard and commercial sour cream. Mound a generous spoonful of chopped, sweet, fresh cucumber pickles on each sandwich; dust with paprika and serve to eat with a fork.

PINEAPPLE-BUTTERMILK SHERBET

Mix together 2 cups cultured buttermilk, ⅔ cup sugar, ¼ teaspoon salt, 1 can (8 oz.) crushed pineapple, and 2 teaspoons vanilla. (If you like a very smooth sherbet, whirl mixture in the blender.)

Pour into a freezer tray and freeze until mushy. Turn into a bowl and whip with a rotary beater until smooth; stir in 1 stiffly beaten egg white. Return to tray and freeze. Makes about 1 quart.

Tongue and Vegetable Soup

This soup takes time to cook, but requires no tending. The first step in preparing the tongue is to cook it in liquid. Here the liquid is enriched with carrots, onions, celery, and seasonings, and the stock becomes an especially mellow and satisfying soup.

If you wish, skin the cooked tongue and make sandwiches to accompany the soup, or use the tongue in any dish calling for this meat.

1 beef tongue (3 to 4 lbs.)
4 cups water
3 medium-sized carrots, cut in large pieces
2 medium-sized onions, cut in large pieces
1 small stalk celery
3 sprigs parsley
1 bay leaf
¼ teaspoon thyme
⅛ teaspoon rosemary
8 or 10 whole black peppers
1½ teaspoons salt
Commercial sour cream

Scrub tongue with a stiff brush and wash well under running water. Place tongue in a deep kettle. Add water, carrots, onions, celery, parsley, bay leaf, thyme, rosemary, whole black peppers, and salt. Bring to a boil, reduce heat. Cover and simmer slowly for 4 hours. Remove tongue, discard bay leaf, and chill stock. Peel skin from tongue and serve the meat, hot or cold, with the soup or for another meal. Remove fat from cold stock. Force vegetables through a wire sieve (or whirl in a blender with some of the stock until smooth). Combine stock with puréed vegetables; heat and serve. Spoon a dollop of sour cream into each bowl. Makes 6 to 8 servings.

Green Soup

You may find this combination of vegetables surprising, but their flavors blend unusually well.

    2 slices bacon
    3 cups water
1½ to 2 cups cooked fresh green limas, chopped
    1 cup raw cauliflower, cut in small pieces
    ½ small onion, thinly sliced
    ¼ teaspoon garlic salt
    ½ teaspoon parsley flakes or 1 teaspoon fresh
        parsley, chopped
    ⅛ teaspoon marjoram
    2 tablespoons flour blended with 2 tablespoons
        water
    Salt and pepper to taste

Cut bacon into 1-inch squares and cook in a large heavy pan until browned; drain off fat. Add the water along with chopped green limas. Add cauliflower, onion, garlic salt, parsley, and marjoram. Cook until the cauliflower is almost tender, about 10 minutes. Gradually stir in the flour and water paste, stirring until thickened and smooth. Add salt and pepper to taste. Continue cooking until cauliflower pieces are tender. Makes about 6 servings. (Instead of fresh limas, you can use 1 package—10 oz.—frozen limas, cooked according to package directions, or 1 can — 1 lb. — green limas. Drain limas and substitute this liquid for an equal quantity of the water.)

Sopa de Mexico

Well seasoned (not "hot") Mexican soup makes a good conversation starter. Chocolate is an unexpected ingredient.

    ¼ cup chopped green pepper
    ¼ cup chopped onions
    ½ clove garlic, minced or mashed
    2 tablespoons butter
    1 can (10½ oz.) condensed beef consommé
1½ cups canned tomato juice
    ¼ teaspoon anise seed
    1 teaspoon sesame seed
    1 teaspoon chile powder
        Dash each ground cloves, cinnamon, and
            pepper
    1 tablespoon grated unsweetened chocolate
    3 tablespoons ground or finely chopped almonds
        Salt to taste

Sauté the green pepper, onion, and garlic in butter over low heat about 5 minutes. Add all the remaining ingredients and simmer for about 20 minutes, or until the vegetables are soft. Pour the mixture into a blender and blend until smooth and creamy. When you are ready to serve, reheat, adding a little water if soup seems too thick; add salt to taste. (If you don't have an electric blender, omit the almonds when you simmer the other ingredients. Press through a wire strainer or food mill; then add the ground almonds just before you reheat the soup.) Makes 4 to 6 servings.

Bacon Vegetable Chowder

Attractive, quick to prepare, and with ingredients that travel well, here is a good soup to serve on a camping trip. If a heavier meal is desired, toast cheese sandwiches in a frying pan.

8 medium-sized potatoes, peeled and cut into
   ½-inch cubes
   Water
8 slices (½ lb.) bacon, cut in 1 or 2-inch lengths
2 large onions, finely chopped
1 can (1 lb.) limas
1 can (1 lb.) cream style corn
1 can (10¾ oz.) condensed tomato soup
4 tablespoons (⅛ lb.) butter or margarine
   Salt and pepper

Place potatoes in a large kettle; barely cover with water and cover; simmer 6 minutes or until potatoes are tender. While potatoes are cooking, fry bacon until half cooked. Add onions and continue cooking until onions are soft and bacon is browned. Pour liquid off potatoes; reserve. Drain limas and add liquid to potato water, adding enough additional water to make 2 cups. Return liquid to potatoes along with onions and bacon, limas, corn, tomato soup, butter, salt and pepper to taste. Stirring occasionally, cook over low heat for 10 minutes. Makes 8 servings.

Smooth cheese soup, pretzels, and peach shortcake make a light lunch suitable for family or guests. Everyone adds his choice of condiments to the soup — green pepper, pimiento, almonds, bacon, popcorn.

Cheese Soup with Condiments

(see suggested menu below)

Each person adds his own selection of condiments to this smooth cheese soup.

        2 tablespoons chopped onion
        2 tablespoons butter
        2 tablespoons flour
        2 chicken bouillon cubes
        6 cups milk
    1¼ cups shredded sharp yellow cheese
        Pinch of dry mustard
        Salt, pepper, paprika
        Condiments: chopped green pepper, thin pi-
            miento strips, toasted slivered almonds,
            crumbled crisp bacon, buttered popcorn

In the top of a double boiler over direct heat, sauté onion in melted butter until golden. Stir in flour and bouillon cubes; blend in milk. Place over hot water and cook until slightly thickened. Add cheese and mustard and continue cooking until cheese melts, stirring occasionally. Season to taste with salt, pepper, and paprika. Serve immediately, adding condiments as desired to each serving. Makes 5 to 6 servings.

Ravioli Soup

Here's an ingenious way to use canned ravioli in a hearty vegetable soup.

        1 can (10½ oz.) condensed beef consommé
        1 cup canned tomato juice
        3 cups water
            About ¾ cup diced carrot
            About ¾ cup diced peeled potato
    ¼ cup chopped green onion
    ¼ cup chopped parsley
        1 teaspoon salt
        1 teaspoon sugar
    ¼ teaspoon pepper
        1 cup chopped fresh spinach
        1 can (about 15 oz.) ravioli
            Grated Parmesan cheese

Combine the consommé, tomato juice, and water in a large pan. Bring to a boil and add the carrot, potato, onion, parsley, salt, sugar, and pepper. Cover and simmer until the vegetables are tender, about 7 minutes. Add the spinach and gently stir in the ravioli, including its sauce. Heat about 10 minutes. Taste, and correct seasoning if needed. Serve with some of the vegetables and ravioli in each bowl. Pass the cheese to sprinkle on each serving. Makes about 6 to 8 servings.

Family or Guest Lunch

Cheese Soup with Condiments
(see recipe above)
Pretzels
Fresh Peach Shortcake

Soup and shortcake make a lunch combination suitable for family or guests in this menu. The golden soup is gaily served in the style of an Indian curry, with five colorful side dishes. The fresh peach shortcake is served with generous swirls of whipped cream.

FRESH PEACH SHORTCAKE

Make your favorite shortcake recipe or follow directions for shortcake on a package of prepared biscuit mix. Shape for individual servings or bake several large layers. Cool. Generously fill and top cake with peach slices and whipped cream.

Meat and Seafood Soups

Hearty Bean Soup *(see suggested menu below)*

1 can (11½ oz.) condensed bean with bacon soup
1 can (10¾ oz.) condensed vegetable bean soup
2 soup cans water
1 cup cubed pasteurized process cheese
3 thinly sliced knackwurst or frankfurters

Empty both soups into a medium-sized pan. Stir water into soups gradually and heat. When soup is steamy, stir in cheese and sausage. Continue heating the soup, stirring occasionally, until the cheese is melted in smoothly. Makes 4 to 6 servings.

Quick Soup Lunch

Hearty Bean Soup *(see recipe above)*
Dilled Deviled Eggs
Oyster Crackers and Rye Wafers
Date Peanut Butter Drops
Tangerines or Oranges
Milk

If the cookies are baked and the eggs hard-cooked in advance, this meal can be prepared in the ten minutes required for the soup to heat.

DILLED DEVILED EGGS

Peel 4 hard-cooked eggs and cut in halves. Carefully remove the yolks; blend until smooth with 2 tablespoons mayonnaise, ½ teaspoon Dijon-style mustard, a dash of pepper, and 2 tablespoons chopped dill pickle. Refill whites with yolk mixture; garnish with parsley. Makes 4 to 6 servings.

DATE PEANUT BUTTER DROPS

2 cups unsifted all-purpose flour
2½ teaspoons baking powder
¼ teaspoon salt
¾ cup soft butter or margarine
¾ cup peanut butter
1¼ cups firmly packed brown sugar
1 teaspoon vanilla
2 eggs
½ cup milk
1 cup packaged chopped dates or sugar-coated chopped dates

Sift together flour, baking powder, and salt. Cream butter, peanut butter, and sugar together until light and fluffy. Blend in vanilla and eggs, beating well. Add flour mixture alternately with milk to creamed mixture. Stir in dates. Drop by heaping teaspoonfuls onto ungreased baking sheets. Bake in a moderate oven (350°) for 15 to 20 minutes or until lightly browned. Makes about 6 dozen cookies.

This family lunch (a good one for Saturday noon) includes hearty bean soup, deviled eggs, crackers, fruit, and cookies. The quick soup combines two different canned soups — bean with bacon, and vegetable bean.

Chicken (or Turkey) Soup

You need the leftover bones or whole carcass of a chicken or turkey to make this soup.

> *Meat and bones from leftover poultry*
> *Water*
> *2 or 3 chicken bouillon cubes (optional)*
> *1 medium-sized onion, chopped*
> *½ green or red pepper, chopped*
> *2 large stalks celery, sliced*
> *1 can (1 lb.) solid pack tomatoes or 1½ cups canned tomato juice*
> *2 tablespoons chopped parsley*
> *2 teaspoons Worcestershire*
> *1 teaspoon seasoning salt*
> *⅓ cup uncooked rice*
> *2 to 4 frozen okra, sliced (optional)*
> *Salt and pepper to taste*

Put the cooked chicken or turkey into a large pan; include also any uncooked parts of the birds, such as necks or backs. Cover with water. Simmer slowly about 2 hours; refrigerate.

When you are ready to make the soup, skim off fat from the stock. Remove the bones and skin, cutting off good meat pieces; reserve meat. Strain stock, measure, and add water if needed to make 2 quarts. Bring to a boil, adding the bouillon cubes only if needed to enrich the stock. Add the onion, green pepper, celery, tomatoes, parsley, Worcestershire, seasoning salt, rice, okra (if used), salt, and pepper. Simmer until vegetables are tender. Makes 8 to 10 servings.

Shrimp Bisque

(see suggested menu below)

Heat 4 cans frozen condensed cream of shrimp soup (10 oz. *each*) according to directions on the can, but use half-and-half (half milk, half cream) instead of milk, and blend in 1 teaspoon anchovy paste. When soup has thawed, whirl smooth in a blender (or force through a food mill) and reheat, adding ½ cup tiny cooked shrimp. Serve at once or keep warm in a tureen over a candle warmer, on an electric warming tray, or in an electric saucepan set at lowest heat. Ladle soup into cups and sprinkle each cup with a few additional tiny shrimp. Makes 12 servings.

Cold Cream of Shrimp Soup

Blend 1 can (10 oz.) frozen condensed cream of shrimp soup, thawed, with ½ soup can milk, ½ soup can water, and 1 or 2 teaspoons lemon juice. Chill about 4 hours. Top with finely minced pimiento or a dash of paprika. Makes 2 to 3 servings.

Seafood Soup

Similar in flavor to cioppino, but easier to serve and eat, seafood soup is delicious accompanied by thin slices of jack cheese melted onto thinly sliced French bread.

Drop-In Luncheon

Shrimp Bisque *(see recipe above)*
Melba Toast
Fruit Salad Bar   Buttermilk Biscuits
Cookies   Schwarzen mit Schlag

Distinguished, but easy to prepare, here is a party luncheon for 12 based on a hearty shrimp bisque which you make from frozen shrimp soup. Guests assemble their own salad from a selection of fresh fruits, crisp greens, and three dressings.

FRUIT SALAD BAR

At the buffet table, arrange a stack of cold plates, a bowl of crisp greens, and platters with these assorted fruits attractively arranged in rows: thin slices of pineapple; slices of peeled oranges, halved; grapes plucked from their stems and seeded, if necessary; sliced pears, bananas, apples, and avocados (dipped in lemon juice or some other anti-darkening agent); and, if you wish, papayas, grapefruit, and persimmons. Serve with a selection of 2 or 3 dressings, such as French-style oil and vinegar, commercial sour cream, and a thin mayonnaise. Let each guest select his own salad combination.

BUTTERMILK BISCUITS

Use ready-to-bake refrigerator biscuits. Get them ready for the oven ahead of time; then bake only as many at one time as you will need for the guests present. If you have a table oven, bake the biscuits right in front of the guests. Serve hot and buttered.

SCHWARZEN MIT SCHLAG (VIENNESE COFFEE)

Serve black coffee in small cups, and top with sweetened whipped cream. Accompany with your favorite dainty cookies.

½ cup diced salt pork
  Hot water
1 tablespoon butter
1 medium-sized onion, diced
2 tablespoons flour
2 cups boiling water
1 can (12 oz.) tomato juice
1 can or bottle (12 oz.) clam juice
1 cup diced celery
½ cup chopped green pepper
2 cups diced potato
½ teaspoon sage
½ teaspoon pepper
1 teaspoon minced fresh or dry thyme
  Salt to taste
1 cup raw crab meat
½ cup shelled raw shrimp
1 jar (10 oz.) small oysters

Scald the pork by covering with hot water for a few minutes; drain. Heat pork with the butter in a large pan; add onion and cook over medium heat until browned. Blend in flour; gradually stir in the water, tomato juice, and clam juice. Add celery, green pepper, potato, and seasonings. Simmer about 30 minutes, or until the vegetables are tender. Add crab and shrimp; simmer 10 minutes more. Add oysters; cook 5 minutes, or until edges curl. Serve in heated bowls. Makes 6 servings.

Quick Lobster Chowder

Sprinkle each serving of this seafood chowder with minced parsley or chives.

1 can (10½ oz.) condensed cream of mushroom
  soup
1 can (10¾ oz.) condensed tomato soup
1¼ cups milk
1 can (6½ oz.) lobster meat
  Minced parsley or chives

Blend together the mushroom soup, tomato soup, and milk; heat until steaming. Add lobster meat and heat through. Garnish with minced parsley or chives. Makes 4 to 6 servings.

Iceberg Soup with Oysters

To those who are addicted to the crisp, fresh tossed salad, the conversion of lettuce to a soup borders on sacrilege. But if you delight in delicate flavors, lettuce soup, served hot or cold, can provide a taste adventure.

1 medium-sized head iceberg lettuce, washed,
  drained, and chopped (about 6 cups)
1 cup diced carrots
½ cup chopped onion
4 tablespoons butter or margarine
1 can (14 oz.) chicken broth
1 cup oysters, fresh or canned
2 tablespoons flour
2 cups milk or half-and-half (half milk,
  half cream)
  Salt
1 to 2 tablespoons lemon juice

Combine chopped lettuce with carrots and onion. Cook in 2 tablespoons of the melted butter until lettuce wilts. Add ½ cup of the chicken broth to the vegetables; save the remainder of broth. Add oysters and cook, covered, until carrots are just barely tender. Whirl mixture smooth in a blender or rub through a fine wire strainer. Blend in remaining chicken broth.

Melt the remaining 2 tablespoons butter in a pan; mix in the flour and gradually add the milk or cream. Cook, stirring, until slightly thickened and simmering. Blend in the lettuce mixture; add salt and the lemon juice to taste. Serve hot or chilled. Makes 6 to 8 servings.

FULL-MEAL FAMILY SOUPS

Just serve with bread

A thick, meat-rich soup full of vegetables is the kind of dish that makes an everyday meal memorable, and it can prove a blessing to a busy cook. This is honest fare, especially suited to family serving; however, it is a rare guest who wouldn't also delight in such food. Serve these hearty soups in big bowls, and you may need a knife and fork to dispose of them properly.

Ham, beef, and lamb, used plentifully, are the bases of the various soups in this chapter. In addition, there are two creamy chowders — one chicken and the other seafood. All of the soups fall into three groups because of the distinct differences in methods of preparation: Some take a long time to cook, simmering away quietly on top of the range and requiring only an occasional stir or glance; some cook in the oven more in the manner of a casserole, usually with ingredients added in stages (such as vegetables, added late to preserve their appearance); a few are really quick to make.

Reheating does no harm to flavor, but if the soup contains green vegetables, they may become drab in color; shellfish may toughen. Dense soups tend to thicken upon standing, and you may have to dilute them with a little broth or water to achieve the desired consistency. On the whole, fresh vegetables are used in these recipes, but some canned and frozen ones do save steps where specified.

With soups like the ones in this chapter, you may wish to serve a favorite bread, a salad, or both. This is a good time to try some of the mixes for fancy muffins or cornbread (cornbread sticks, too), or frozen bakery items like brioche, croissants, or special dinner rolls. An unfailingly popular choice is fresh, crusty French bread. If you serve a dessert, ice cream or fruit is an appropriate climax when it's "soup for dinner."

Well seasoned by two additions of onions, the rich beef broth of this onion soup blends harmoniously with melting cheese. Recipe given on page 77.

Cabbage and Ham Soup

(see suggested menu below)

To preserve its bright green color, cook the cabbage last.

¼ cup diced green pepper
¼ cup diced celery
½ cup diced onion
2 tablespoons chopped parsley
3 tablespoons butter
2 cups diced cooked ham (a little less than 1 lb.)
1 bay leaf
2 tablespoons flour
1 tablespoon chicken stock concentrate
3 cups cold water
2 cups finely shredded cabbage
1 tablespoon water
   About 1 cup commercial sour cream

In a wide frying pan, cook the green pepper, celery, onion, and parsley in 2 tablespoons of the butter until they are soft, but not browned. Add the ham and bay leaf; cook until ham is heated through. Blend in the flour, chicken stock concentrate, and the 3 cups cold water; pour into pan with ham. Bring to a boil, stirring, and simmer a minute or two. Pour into a tureen or individual serving bowls and keep in a warm place.

In the same frying pan, melt the remaining 1 tablespoon butter over highest heat and add the cabbage and 1 tablespoon water. Cook, stirring, until cabbage turns brighter in color and softens slightly. Mix into soup. Pass sour cream and spoon some into each serving. Makes 4 generous servings.

Ham Hocks with Lima Beans

Prepare this very thick ham and bean dish in the oven. Accompany it with a green salad and hot, home-baked rolls.

2 cups dry lima beans
   Water
4 ham hocks
2 bay leaves
1 large onion, chopped
½ green pepper, sliced in rounds
1 can (1 lb.) solid pack tomatoes
1 can (8 oz.) tomato sauce
1 tablespoon salt
¼ teaspoon pepper
¼ teaspoon ground cloves

Cabbage and Ham Soup Supper

Cabbage and Ham Soup
(see recipe above)

| Hot Cornbread | Boysenberry Jam |
| Winter Pears | Fontinella Cheese |

The quick-cooking, ham-rich soup goes together after you put cornbread (made from a mix or your favorite recipe) in to bake. Serve boysenberry jam with the cornbread; pass a bowl of sour cream for each person to spoon into his bowl of soup. A simple dessert of winter pears and fontinella cheese completes the menu.

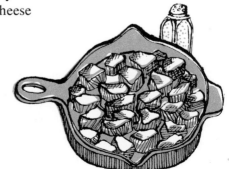

Soak the beans in water to cover overnight (or if your time is limited, cover them with water; boil briskly 2 minutes; then remove from heat and soak only 1 hour). Without draining the beans, add ham hocks, bay leaves, and water — if needed to cover the beans again. Simmer about 1 hour or until beans are tender. Add the onion, green pepper, tomatoes, tomato sauce, salt, pepper, and cloves. Mix until blended and pour into a large (4-quart) casserole. Cover and bake in a moderate oven (350°) about 1 hour, or until the meat is tender. Remove meat from beans; chop meat and discard bones and fat, if you wish; return meat to soup before you serve it. Makes 6 servings.

Broccoli-Ham Soup

Thick with meat and vegetables, you can make broccoli-ham soup from basic ingredients in a surprisingly short time.

½ cup finely chopped ham
2 cloves garlic, minced
2 tablespoons olive oil or other salad oil
1 cup canned, solid pack tomatoes
1 package (10 oz.) frozen chopped broccoli (or about 2 cups chopped fresh broccoli)
½ teaspoon nutmeg
4 cups chicken or beef bouillon, made from cubes or stock concentrate (or 2 cans condensed beef bouillon, diluted with water to make 4 cups)
½ cup uncooked elbow, shell, or spiral macaroni
Salt and pepper to taste
Grated Parmesan cheese

In a 2-quart pan, sauté the chopped ham and garlic in olive oil until delicately browned. Add the tomatoes, broccoli, nutmeg, and bouillon; simmer for about 20 minutes. Add the uncooked macaroni and continue cooking for 5 to 10 minutes, or until macaroni is tender. Add salt and pepper to taste. Serve in hot bowls, and pass grated Parmesan cheese to sprinkle on top, if you wish. Makes 6 generous servings.

Onion Soup with Port

Exceptionally full flavored, this onion and beef soup should be served in wide bowls to be eaten with a knife and fork, as well as a big soup spoon. If you have a handsome tureen, by all means serve the soup from it, or simply fill bowls from the simmering kettle.

A meal like this needs only a salad of greens served before or with the soup; a bread, such as toasted, buttered English muffins; and a dessert, such as apple pie or a sweet soufflé.

4 slices meaty beef shank, each about 1 inch thick
6 large onions, chopped
10 cups water
About 1½ teaspoons salt
1 bay leaf
2 egg whites, beaten until frothy (optional)
4 large onions, sliced
4 tablespoons butter, melted
2 to 3 tablespoons white port
Shredded Gruyère or Danish Samsoe cheese

Place the beef shanks in a large pan and add the chopped onions, water, salt, and bay leaf. Bring mixture to a boil; cover and simmer for about 2½ hours. Discard bones and fat; set meat aside. Strain broth; discard onions, bay leaf.

If desired, clarify the broth in this manner: Bring broth to a boil and vigorously beat in the egg whites (use a wire whip or rotary beater). Take pan from heat and let broth settle for one or two minutes. Moisten a muslin cloth (dish towel) in cold water and wring dry. Line a large strainer with cloth and pour broth through. Discard egg white. Lightly brown sliced onions in melted butter. Add broth and simmer for 10 minutes or until onions are tender. Add meat, and wine and salt to taste. Ladle soup into bowls; spoon shredded cheese into each serving. Makes 6 to 8 servings.

Mexican Albóndigas Soup

A clear consommé touched with sherry forms the base of one version of Mexican meatball soup. The little meatballs are filled with pine nuts instead of the more typical rice.

 1 pound ground beef round
 ¾ teaspoon salt
 ¾ teaspoon chile powder
 1 small onion, grated
 1 cup fine dry bread crumbs
 ½ cup pine nuts
 1 egg, slightly beaten
 2 cans (10½ oz. each) condensed beef consommé
 2 soup cans water
 1 bay leaf
 ¼ cup dry sherry

Mix together ground round, salt, chile powder, onion, bread crumbs, pine nuts and egg. Shape into tiny meatballs about 1 inch or less in diameter. Pour consommé, water, and bay leaf into a pan; cover and bring to a boil. Add meatballs, a few at a time so that boiling is constant. Reduce heat, cover, and simmer for 30 minutes. Just before serving, remove the bay leaf and stir in the sherry. Makes 4 to 6 servings.

Cabbage Borsch

Serve this meat and vegetable soup for supper with sour rye bread. You might garnish each bowl with a large spoonful of sour cream.

 3 to 4 pounds short ribs of beef
 3 quarts water
 4 teaspoons salt
 4 whole black peppers
 1 bay leaf
 1 to 2 bunches unpeeled beets, cut in large dice
 2 large carrots, cut in ¾-inch slices
 2 stalks celery, cut in ½-inch slices
 1 medium-sized potato, cut in large dice
 1 large onion, cut in large dice
 1 can (1 lb.) solid pack tomatoes
 1 small head cabbage
 2 tablespoons lemon juice
 1 tablespoon sugar

In a large pan, put meat, water, salt, peppers, and bay leaf; bring to a boil and simmer for 1 hour. Add beets and cook 1 more hour. Remove meat from broth with a slotted spoon; set aside. Add carrots, celery, potato, and onion. Drain liquid from canned tomatoes into soup; chop tomatoes and add. Cut meat from bones, discard fat and bone, and add meat to soup; simmer about 1 hour longer. You can do this much ahead. About 20 minutes before serving, reheat to boiling. Cut cabbage into 1-inch wedges and remove core; add cabbage to soup and simmer about 10 minutes. Stir in lemon juice and sugar just before serving. Makes 12 generous servings.

Eggplant Supper Soup

Eggplant supper soup resembles minestrone.

 2 tablespoons olive oil or salad oil
 2 tablespoons butter or margarine
 1 medium-sized onion, chopped
 1 pound lean ground beef
 1 medium-sized eggplant, diced
 1 clove garlic, minced or mashed
 ½ cup chopped carrot
 ½ cup sliced celery
 1 large can (1 lb., 12 oz.) pear-shaped tomatoes
 2 cans (14 oz. each) beef broth
 1 teaspoon salt
 1 teaspoon sugar
 ½ teaspoon pepper
 ½ teaspoon nutmeg
 ½ cup salad macaroni
 2 tablespoons minced parsley
   Grated Parmesan cheese

Heat the salad oil and butter in a large pan or Dutch oven, add the onion, and sauté until limp, about 3 minutes. Add the meat and stir over the heat until it loses its pinkness. Add the eggplant, garlic, carrots, celery, tomatoes (break up tomatoes with a fork), beef broth, salt, sugar, pepper, and nutmeg. Cover and simmer for about 30 minutes. Add the macaroni and parsley and simmer about 10 minutes more, or until macaroni is tender. Serve in large heated soup bowls. Pass the Parmesan cheese to sprinkle over each serving of soup at the table. Makes 6 to 8 large servings.

Beef and Sauerkraut Soup *(see suggested menu below)*

Beef shanks fortify this substantial soup.

> 4 beef shanks, about 1½ inches thick (2½ to 3 lbs.)
> 1 tablespoon butter
> 1 tablespoon salad oil
> 1 large onion, finely chopped
> 1 can (1 lb.) sauerkraut
> 4 cups water
> 1 can (1 lb.) solid pack tomatoes
> 10 whole black peppers
> 1 bay leaf
>   About ¾ teaspoon salt
>   Commercial sour cream

Trim off any fat from edges of beef shanks; discard. Brown beef on both sides in butter and oil in a large heavy pan. Reduce heat, add onion, and cook until they are limp. Add sauerkraut with its liquid, water, and tomatoes. Tie peppers and bay leaf in cheesecloth; add to pan. Bring sauerkraut mixture to a boil; reduce heat, cover, and simmer about 2½ hours or until meat is very tender.

Remove meat with a slotted spoon; cut into bite-sized pieces, discarding bones, and return meat to soup. Discard cheesecloth packet of seasonings. Add salt to taste, if needed. Cut through sauerkraut several times with kitchen scissors to shorten the strands. Serve with sour cream to spoon over each serving. Makes 4 servings.

 Family Soup Supper

Beef and Sauerkraut Soup
(see recipe above)
Crisp Carrot and Turnip Sticks
Sweet Pickles
Rye or Pumpernickel Bread
Baked Taffy Apples   Cream

The accompaniments for beef and sauerkraut soup are simple — crisp relishes, dark bread, and baked apples. The soup requires 2 to 3 hours of slow cooking, but no attention during that period. You can have the apples ready in advance for the oven; then bake them during dinner.

BAKED TAFFY APPLES

Place ½ cup heavy cream, 20 plain vanilla caramels (about ¾-inch square size), and ¼ teaspoon cinnamon in top of a double boiler over simmering water. Cook, stirring occasionally, until mixture is smooth. Peel and core 4 large baking apples (Winesaps or Rome Beauties). Place in a buttered 8-inch-square baking pan. Fill centers of apples with ½ cup chopped, pitted dates; dot with a total of 1 tablespoon butter. Spoon caramel mixture evenly over apples. Cover with foil, and bake in a moderate oven (350°) for about 45 minutes, or until apples are just tender. Remove apples to individual serving dishes. Stir sauce in pan until smooth; spoon over each serving. If you wish, serve with a pitcher of plain heavy cream or cream whipped just until foamy. Makes 4 servings.

Lamb in vegetable soup need not be reserved for the family; it is an elegant and simple way to entertain guests with a dish that's a full meal. Simply serve with good French bread.

Lamb and Sausage Soup

A final aromatic touch is the addition of red wine to each serving of lamb and sausage soup.

1 package (12 oz.) dried lentils
2 medium-sized carrots
3 medium-sized onions
9 cups water
  About 1½ teaspoons salt
4 lamb shanks
¾-pound ham hock
1 cup dry red wine
6 to 8 garlic sausages
  Dry red wine

Wash lentils in cold water and drain well; place in a large pan. Coarsely dice the carrots, and chop the onions. Add carrots, onions, water, and the salt to the lentils. Bring this mixture to a boil and add the lamb shanks, ham hock, and 1 cup of the dry red table wine. Cover and simmer gently for about 2½ hours or until meats are very tender. If you wish, remove bones and fat from meats and discard; skim excess fat from surface of soup.

Add the garlic sausages, whole or cut in thick slices, and simmer soup for about 20 minutes more. Ladle soup into large serving bowls and add about 1 tablespoon of the red wine (a small decanter for the wine makes it easier to serve) to each bowl, if desired. Makes 6 to 8 servings.

Lamb and Pea Soup

Lamb shanks, wine, herbs, and peas contribute to the flavor of this soup. The shanks are served separately. To reheat them, place in a covered casserole with ¼ cup water or red table wine. Bake in a moderate oven (350°) for 20 minutes.

4 lamb shanks
¾ cup dry red wine
3½ cups water
1 medium-sized onion, cut in pieces
3 or 4 sprigs parsley
1 bay leaf
1½ teaspoons summer savory
10 whole black peppers
1½ teaspoons salt
3 cups fresh or frozen peas
Sautéed small whole mushrooms

Place shanks in a deep kettle. Add wine, water, onion, parsley, bay leaf, savory, whole black peppers, and salt. Bring to a boil; reduce heat. Cover and simmer slowly for 3 hours. Remove shanks from stock and chill until ready to reheat and serve. Strain stock and chill. When cold, discard fat layer. Force peas through a wire strainer (or whirl in a blender with some of stock until smooth, then pour through wire strainer). Blend with stock, bring to a boil, and simmer 3 or 4 minutes. Serve hot, garnished with sautéed mushrooms. Heat shanks as directed above and serve as an accompaniment. Makes 6 or 8 servings.

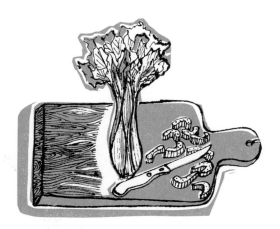

Lamb in Vegetable Soup

Colorful and attractive, lamb in vegetable soup has been adapted from a traditional Basque dish. If you have your own vegetable garden, it would be a delightful way to show off some of the small, tender vegetables for a company meal. To coax extraordinary flavors from the ingredients, you brown all the meats and some of the vegetables before cooking them in liquid.

6 thin slices bacon
½ pound ham, diced, or cut in 1-inch squares
2 pounds lamb stew meat, cut in 1-inch cubes
1 large onion, sliced
5 or 6 carrots, quartered (or equivalent in small whole carrots)
12 small whole boiling onions
1 tablespoon flour
1 large can (1 qt., 15 oz.) chicken stock
1½ cups water
8 to 12 small whole new potatoes
2 celery tops
3 large leaves lettuce
1 cup fresh or frozen asparagus tips
1 cup fresh or frozen peas
1 cup fresh or frozen artichoke hearts
Boiling salted water
3 hard-cooked eggs, quartered (optional)

Cook the bacon in a large frying pan; remove when crisp, leaving the fat in pan. Sauté ham in the bacon fat until browned on all sides. Crumble bacon and put into a Dutch oven or large (about 4-quart) earthenware casserole with the ham. In the same frying pan, sauté the lamb pieces until well browned; transfer to the casserole. Add the sliced onion, carrots, and boiling onions to the same cooking fat, and cook until they are nicely browned on all sides. Remove carrots and whole onions to the casserole with meats. Drain the fat from the frying pan, leaving in browned onion slices. Blend the flour with the onions in pan, gradually stir in the stock and water, and bring to a boil. Pour liquid through a wire strainer into the casserole with meat and vegetables; discard sliced onion. Also put into the casserole the whole potatoes, celery tops, and lettuce; cover and bake in a moderately hot oven (375°) until tender, about 1 hour. (If you prefer, simmer the soup gently on top of your range.) Cook the asparagus, peas, and artichokes separately in boiling salted water just until tender, and add to the soup just before you serve it. If you wish, adorn the soup plates with garnish of hard-cooked egg quarters. Makes about 8 generous servings.

Chicken Chowder

(see suggested menu below)

Thick chicken chowder travels well in a vacuum bottle if you elect to serve it at a picnic.

1 stewing chicken (about 4 lbs.), cut up
1 bay leaf
1 carrot
1 clove garlic
  Celery leaves from several stalks of celery
1 or 2 sprigs parsley
1 tablespoon salt
½ teaspoon sage
1 quart water
2 tablespoons chicken fat or butter
1 medium-sized onion, diced
4 medium-sized potatoes, diced
2 cups half-and-half (half milk, half cream)
½ teaspoon thyme
  Salt and freshly ground pepper

Wash chicken and put in large pan with bay leaf, carrot, garlic, celery leaves, parsley, salt, and sage. Add water; cover and simmer until tender, about 2 hours. Cool chicken in stock. Remove meat from bones and cut chicken in bite-sized pieces (about 3½ cups); discard bones and skin.

Skim fat from broth and use 2 tablespoons to brown onion and potato; discard remaining fat. Meanwhile, pour chicken stock through a wire strainer and add 2 cups of it (save remainder for other uses) to potatoes and cook until they are tender. Add chicken pieces, half-and-half, thyme, salt, and pepper to taste. Bring to simmering point, but do not boil. Add a little water if chowder seems too thick. Serve at once or ladle into a 2-quart vacuum bottle (warmed first with hot water) and serve later at a picnic. Makes 6 generous servings.

Finnish Fish Chowder

This dish can be made with fillet from salmon or almost any other fish.

½ cup (¼ lb.) butter or margarine
4 medium-sized potatoes, peeled and thinly sliced
2 medium-sized onions, thinly sliced
  About 1½ teaspoons salt
  About ¼ teaspoon pepper
2 bay leaves, finely crushed
¼ teaspoon ground allspice
  About 1½ pounds fish fillets

Cook this on top of your range in a utensil attractive enough to come to the table, or use an

---

Hot Chowder Picnic

Hot Chicken Chowder
(see recipe above)
Buttered French Bread
Radishes   Carrot Sticks   Celery
Devil's Food Cake
Hot Coffee

Vacuum bottles make this cool weather picnic feasible. It is easy to ladle the chowder from a wide-mouth jug into paper or plastic bowls; be sure to bring spoons for the thick soup. Use a wide-mouth vacuum bottle, partially filled with ice, as a crisping container for the raw vegetable relishes. Bake the cake in one layer from a mix. Make sure the bottle for coffee holds a generous supply.

electric frying pan. Melt 2 tablespoons of the butter in the bottom of the cooking utensil; remove from heat. Arrange half the potatoes in the bottom of the pan. Cover with half the onions. Combine the salt, pepper, bay, and allspice; sprinkle about ⅓ of the mixture over onions. Make a layer of the fish fillets; sprinkle with ⅓ of the spice. Make a layer of remaining potatoes, then a top layer of onions. Sprinkle with the remaining spice. Dot the top with the rest of the butter. Cover the pan and place over lowest heat for about 2 hours, or until the potatoes are tender (or cook it in an electric pan set at 175°). Makes 4 to 6 servings.

Seafood Chowder

This chowder is ideal for an impromptu picnic, as it cooks quickly over a fire. It is equally memorable for a fine meal at home; just add salad, French bread, beverages, and dessert. On a picnic, plan to complete food preparation at the site, and delegate some of the duties.

THE BROTH:

 4 large onions, chopped
 2 or 3 stalks celery, sliced
 2 bay leaves
 ½ cup (¼ lb.) butter
 2 cans (6 or 8 oz. each) whole mushrooms and liquid
 4 cans (14 oz. each) chicken broth
   About 1½ cups dry white wine
 3 cups heavy cream

THE FISH:

2 or 3 spiny lobsters (frozen thawed), split lengthwise
2 Dungeness (market) crabs (live, cooked, or frozen thawed), cleaned and cracked
 2 pounds skinned, boned rockfish or halibut, cut into large chunks
 1 pound large shrimp in shells
6 or 8 medium-sized sole fillets
 4 slices frozen abalone, thawed and cut into chunks (optional)

In a large deep pan (at least 3-gallon size) combine onions, celery, bay leaves, and butter and cook over hot fire or high heat, stirring, until butter melts; then cover pan and simmer until vegetables are soft, stirring occasionally. Add mushrooms and liquid, broth, wine, and cream; stir well, cover, and bring to boiling.

When you buy the fish, have the lobsters split, crabs cracked and cleaned, and the rockfish or halibut boned and skinned. Cut up rest of fish at the picnic or at home. To devein shrimp, slip a slender wooden or metal skewer into the back of each shrimp just below the vein, pulling up through shell to draw out vein; repeat in several places along back to remove all the vein.

If lobster and crab are uncooked, add to broth, cover and cook 10 minutes. If they are cooked, or cooked, frozen and thawed, then add to pan along with rockfish, shrimp, and sole. Push fish well down into liquid. Cover and cook over the hot fire for 5 to 8 minutes or until returned to full boil. Stir in abalone, if you use it, and remove pan from heat. Cover and let stand undisturbed 2 or 3 minutes.

To serve fish, lift it from chowder with a strainer ladle or slotted spoon. Strip meat from lobster shells and divide into serving-size pieces. Make sure each person gets a sampling of all the fish at first or second servings. After the fish is served, ladle the broth into cups for sipping. Makes 10 generous or 12 adequate servings.

MAIN-DISH STEWS

For the family or unexpected guests

The plainest of stews can be a work of art and a pleasure to the eye as well as the taste buds. But the coarser, more fibrous cuts of meat don't become tender, succulent morsels with haphazard treatment, nor does the making of a good stew demand a great deal of effort.

The usual, though not invariable, routine is to brown the meat in a little fat, add liquid such as water, tomatoes, yogurt, broth, or canned soup, and simmer gently in the oven or on top of the range until the meat is very easy to pierce with a fork or knife tip. Vegetables, in large or small quantities and in variety, are added at almost any point.

The simmering step is the most critical. The liquid around the meat should gently surge and bubble sporadically. Never let the boil become vigorous; too rapid heat at this stage makes the meat irrevocably tough regardless of how long you cook it; instead of becoming tender, it will fall apart and taste dry and stringy.

In this chapter, beef and lamb are used predominately with only brief attention to pork and venison. One interesting stewing method calls for a well seasoned tomato sauce, made in quantity, as the cooking medium for several types of meat; the results in each recipe are refreshingly dissimilar.

The kind and cut of the meat affect the length of cooking time required. For best results, you will always have to test the meat for tenderness, using the specified cooking time more as a suggestion than as an absolute direction.

With a dish like stew, you don't need much else on the menu. A simple salad of cabbage, lettuce, mixed greens, assorted raw vegetables, or marinated cooked vegetables, or just good bread will be adequate. One of the really basic pleasures of stew is soaking up the delicious sauce with a mild starch dish like rice, potatoes (mashed, baked, or boiled new potatoes), cracked wheat, wide or narrow noodles. Let the dessert be a family favorite, with something a little fancier if there is to be company for this comfortable kind of meal.

Stews reheat, benefiting in flavor to some ways of thinking, but often at the sacrifice of appearance.

Plump mushroom caps, browned onions, and a bit of orange peel impart flavor to this succulent beef stew in red wine. For recipe, see page 87.

Beef Mushroom Stew

(see suggested menu below)

Refrigerated biscuits are baked on the top of beef mushroom stew.

>   2 pounds beef stew meat
>   About 2 tablespoons flour
>   3 tablespoons salad oil or shortening
>   2 teaspoons salt
>   ½ teaspoon pepper
>   6 small potatoes, diced
>   6 medium-sized carrots, cut into chunks
>   4 large onions, quartered
>   ¼ cup soy sauce
>   1 cup water
>   1 can (10½ oz.) condensed cream of
>   mushroom soup
>   2 tablespoons lemon juice
>   1 package (8 oz.) refrigerated biscuits (about 12
>   biscuits)

Roll meat chunks in flour to coat each piece lightly. Heat the salad oil or shortening in a heavy pan with a cover; brown the meat, stirring constantly. Season with salt and pepper.

Add the potatoes, carrots, and onions to the meat. Then add soy sauce and water. Cover and simmer for 1 hour. Uncover and add cream of mushroom soup and lemon juice. Arrange refrigerated biscuits over top; bake, uncovered, in a hot oven (400°) for 10 minutes or until biscuits are browned. Makes 6 servings.

Paprika Goulash

Beef brisket (instead of the usual stew meat), liver, and paprika elevate this genuine Hungarian goulash well above an ordinary stew. The sauce is thin, so bowls for individual service are best.

>   1 large onion, diced
>   1 tablespoon butter
>   1 tablespoon bacon drippings
>   3 pounds fresh beef brisket, cut in 1-inch cubes
>   ¼ pound calf liver, cut in ½-inch-wide strips
>   2 teaspoons Hungarian paprika or regular
>   paprika
>   1 tablespoon flour
>   1 cup condensed beef consommé
>   1 medium-sized green pepper, minced
>   2½ cups diced, hot cooked potatoes
>   2 medium-sized tomatoes, peeled, seeded,
>   and diced

In a large, heavy pan, lightly brown onion in butter and bacon drippings. Add brisket and liver and brown on all sides. Sprinkle with paprika and

 **Family Dinner**

Beef Mushroom Stew with Baked Dumplings
(see recipe above)
Red Cabbage Slaw
Lemon Sherbet with Frozen Strawberries

You can make the stew early in the day and reheat it before placing the refrigerated biscuits on top to bake; serve as you would stew with dumplings.

Use red cabbage in your favorite slaw recipe. For dessert, cover servings of lemon sherbet with fresh or thawed, sliced strawberries.

flour, and blend in consommé. Cover and simmer very slowly for 1 hour, stirring occasionally. Remove liver and mince, then return to pan along with green pepper. Simmer 1 hour longer, or until meat is tender. Add potatoes and tomatoes, heat through. Makes 8 to 10 servings.

Oven Beef Stew

Your oven does the messy job of browning the meat and stewing it without close supervision.

> 2 pounds beef stew meat
> 2 teaspoons salt
>   Flour
> 1½ cups water
> 6 carrots, cut in large pieces
> ½ pound mushrooms, whole or large pieces
> 10 small onions, whole
> ½ cup chopped parsley
>   Chopped parsley for garnish

Sprinkle meat with salt, then dust with flour, shaking off excess. Arrange pieces in an ungreased baking pan, keeping them slightly separated. Bake in a very hot oven (500°) for 20 minutes.

Remove from oven and pour water into pan, stirring to scrape free the browned particles. Add carrots, mushrooms, onions, and ½ cup chopped parsley. Cover pan tightly with lid or foil, and bake in a moderately hot oven (375°) for 2½ hours,

or until meat is very tender; stir once or twice while cooking. Garnish with more chopped parsley. Makes 4 or 5 servings.

Beef Stew in Red Wine

A strip of orange peel imparts a fruity sweet flavor to the meat in this stew.

> 4 strips bacon, each cut in 1-inch pieces
> 2½ pounds beef stew meat
>   Salt and pepper to taste
> ½ pound small boiling onions
> 3 tablespoons flour
> 1½ cups dry red wine
> 3 tablespoons brandy or cognac
> 2 cloves garlic, minced or mashed
> ⅛ teaspoon marjoram
> ⅛ teaspoon thyme
> 1 strip orange peel from a large orange (pare with a vegetable peeler)
> 1 tablespoon beef stock base plus 1 cup water
> 1 medium-sized onion
> 4 whole cloves
> ½ pound mushrooms
> 2 tablespoons butter or margarine
>   Finely chopped parsley

Brown bacon in a heavy frying pan and remove meat. Season beef with salt and pepper; add to the hot bacon drippings and brown on all sides. Transfer meat and crisp bacon to a 3-quart ovenproof casserole. Add small onions to the drippings and brown lightly; set aside. Sprinkle flour into the drippings and let brown slightly. Gradually stir in wine and brandy. Add garlic, marjoram, thyme, orange peel, beef stock base, water, and the medium-sized onion stuck with cloves. Bring to a boil and pour over meat.

Cover casserole and place in a moderately slow oven (325°) for 2 to 2½ hours, or until meat is almost tender enough to serve. Add the browned onions and cook 30 minutes longer, or until meat is very tender when pierced. Quarter the mushrooms if they are large, or leave whole if small; sauté quickly in the butter. Add the mushrooms to the meat the last 10 or 15 minutes of cooking. Sprinkle with parsley. Makes 6 to 8 servings.

Curried Beef with Vegetables

Serve this curry-flavored stew with rice and your favorite condiments, such as toasted shredded coconut, salted peanuts, butter-fried raisins, and chutney.

> 2 slices bacon, cut in small pieces
> 2 tablespoons butter or margarine
> 1 medium-sized onion, sliced
> 2 pounds round steak, cut in 1-inch cubes
> ½ cup flour
> 1 teaspoon salt
> ¼ teaspoon pepper
> 1½ tablespoons curry powder
>   Water
> 2 bay leaves
> 1 cup diced celery
> 1 cup diced carrots
> 2 cups cubed potatoes
> 1 cup fresh or frozen green peas
> 1 tablespoon lemon juice
>   Flour-and-water paste for thickening

In a heavy kettle or Dutch oven, cook bacon, butter, and onion until the onion is golden brown. Remove onion and bacon with a slotted spoon; set aside. Dredge the meat in the flour mixed with salt, pepper, and curry powder; brown well in the fat remaining in the pan. Sprinkle meat with any of the flour mixture left over; add water to cover, bay leaves, and the onion and bacon. Simmer for 1 hour, or until meat is nearly tender, adding more water if needed. Add celery, carrots, and potatoes, and cook until vegetables are done and meat is tender. Add the peas during the last 10 minutes. Remove the bay leaves; add lemon juice and thicken the gravy, if desired. Makes 6 servings.

German-Style Short Ribs

For best results, allow time for the meat to cook, cool, and be reheated.

> 2½ to 3 pounds short ribs of beef, cut
> 2 tablespoons flour
> 1 teaspoon salt
> ⅛ teaspoon pepper
> 2 tablespoons shortening
> 2 medium-sized onions, sliced
> 1 cup dry red wine
> ½ cup chile sauce or catsup
> 3 tablespoons brown sugar
> 3 tablespoons vinegar
> 1 tablespoon Worcestershire
> ½ teaspoon dry mustard
> ½ teaspoon chile powder
> 1½ tablespoons flour
> ½ cup water

Roll the short ribs in 2 tablespoons flour, combined with salt and pepper, to coat all sides. Melt shortening in a Dutch oven or large heavy pan; add short ribs and cook slowly until well browned all over. Add onions and brown lightly. Then add the wine, chile sauce, brown sugar, vinegar, Worcestershire, mustard, and chile powder. Cover and cook over low heat until the meat is tender, about 2 hours. Remove from heat; cool and refrigerate until needed. Then lift off all the solidified fat. Stir in the 1½ tablespoons flour blended with water. Cook until thickened and meat is heated through. Makes about 4 servings.

Sherried Oxtails

Serve savory oxtail stew with a green salad that includes sliced oranges and red onion rings. Mashed potatoes also make a good accompaniment; for color and flavor, cook and mash 1 carrot with every 3 potatoes. Round out the meal with broccoli spears and dark rye bread. For dessert, provide crisp apples, salted almonds, and slivered crystallized ginger.

¼ cup flour
1 teaspoon salt
3 teaspoons paprika
4 pounds oxtails, cut in serving-sized pieces
¼ cup butter or margarine
2 cups boiling water
½ pound mushrooms, sliced
1 red pepper, thinly sliced and seeded (or 2 canned pimientos, drained and sliced)
2 large onions, thinly sliced
1 clove garlic, mashed
2 beef bouillon cubes
2 vegetable bouillon cubes
3 teaspoons curry powder
1 cup dry sherry or tomato juice

Blend the flour, salt, and paprika. Coat the oxtails with the flour mixture; reserve remaining flour. In a large frying pan with a lid, melt the butter. Brown the floured oxtails in melted butter on all sides. Add boiling water. Cover and simmer the oxtails for about an hour. Stir in the mushrooms, red pepper, onions, garlic, beef and vegetable bouillon cubes, and curry powder. Cover again and continue cooking for about 2 hours longer, or until meat is very tender. Blend in sherry or tomato juice and simmer, uncovered, for about 15 minutes longer. Gradually stir a little of the cooking liquid into the reserved seasoned flour in a small bowl to form a smooth paste; blend flour paste into oxtails and cook, stirring constantly, until thickened and bubbling. Makes 4 to 6 servings.

Sherried oxtails are served with plenty of rich, curry flavored gravy to spoon over mashed potatoes. A green vegetable, crisp salad, and hearty rye bread complete this colorful meal.

Laban Oumu (Lamb and Yogurt Stew)

The meat in laban oumu is moist and mild, with a definite tang of yogurt in the plentiful sauce.

    2 pounds lean lamb, cut in chunks
      Water
    1 teaspoon salt
    2 pounds onions, peeled and cut in chunks
    2 tablespoons cornstarch
    ½ cup water
    3 cups yogurt
      Hot cooked rice or quick-cooking cracked
        wheat
      Chopped mint

Just cover the lamb with water. Add the salt; bring to a boil and skim; add the onions. Simmer for 30 minutes, or until just tender. In another pan, blend the cornstarch with the ½ cup cold water and beat in yogurt until smooth. Simmer, stirring, until thickened. Add the meat mixture and continue to simmer until very tender, about 30 minutes longer. Serve with rice or cracked wheat. Sprinkle with mint. Makes about 6 servings.

Sour Cream Lamb Stew

Canned tomato soup is the base for the fine flavored sauce of the following recipe.

    1 large onion, sliced
    2 or 3 tablespoons butter
    2½ to 3 pounds lamb stew meat
    2 teaspoons salt
      Flour
    1 can (about 10¾ oz.) condensed tomato soup
    1½ cups water
    ½ teaspoon ground ginger
    1 cup (½ pt.) commercial sour cream
    6 to 8 ounces egg noodles, cooked and hot

Cook the onion in butter until soft. Sprinkle the meat with salt; then coat pieces with flour, shaking off excess. Brown the meat lightly on all sides in the pan with the onion. Blend tomato soup with the water and ginger. Pour over meat; blend. Cover and simmer gently for about 2 hours, or until meat is very tender. Stir occasionally and add a little water if sauce begins to stick.

Just before serving, blend some of the hot sauce with the sour cream and return cream to the pan. Do not boil, but heat through. Serve stew with hot cooked egg noodles. Makes 6 servings.

Lamb Stew

(see suggested menu opposite)

Hearty chunks of lamb are cooked with tomatoes, green pepper, celery, onion, and green beans in this Assyrian dish, called *khuroosh*. The method of cooking the vegetables with the meat to mingle flavors and retain all the cooking liquids is traditional. The stew should be cooked until the sauce loses its soupy consistency.

    2½ to 3 pounds boneless lamb shoulder, cut in
        1½-inch chunks
    2 medium-sized onions, peeled
    1 teaspoon paprika
    6 medium-sized tomatoes, peeled
    1 medium-sized green pepper, slivered
    1 stalk celery, chopped
    2 tablespoons chopped parsley
    1½ teaspoons salt
      Dash pepper
    ½ cup water
    2 packages (10 oz. each) frozen cut green beans,
        thawed

Trim fat and outer skin from the meat. Melt some of the fat in a deep pan, and brown the meat in it. Chop one of the onions and cook it with the meat until soft. Drain off the fat, stir in paprika, and cook for about 5 minutes more. Add the remaining whole onion, tomatoes, green pepper, celery, parsley, salt, pepper, and water; cover, bring to a boil, and then reduce heat so mixture simmers. Remove cover and continue cooking, stirring occasionally, for about 1 hour or until lamb is nearly tender and sauce is reduced and thickened. Add the beans, cover again, and simmer the stew for about 30 minutes longer or until both the meat and beans are tender. Makes 6 to 8 servings.

Assyrian Dinner

Lamb Stew *(see recipe opposite)*
Assyrian Rice   Glazed Prunes
Lettuce Wedges with Oil-Lemon Dressing
Fresh Fruits
Coffee

Assyria is a culture without a country. Descendants of this ancient civilization, however, can be found throughout the Middle East, and their foods retain certain distinct elements. The foods in this family style menu consequently reflect not only Assyrian cuisine, but those of such neighboring countries as Iran, Turkey, and Armenia.

The full-bodied sauce of the stew complements the Assyrian rice. To make the rice fluffy with distinct kernels, you soak it overnight, boil it briefly, then finish it in the oven. Butter is used generously to flavor the rice.

The salad is simply lettuce wedges with an herb-seasoned oil and lemon juice dressing.

Glazed prunes with an almost candied consistency are the final element in the main part of the meal. Cooked with lemon slices, the prunes are a piquant contrast to the lamb and rice.

Fresh fruit is ample for dessert. Depending upon the season, you might serve tangerines, bananas, grapes, melon, or apricots.

Finish the rice and prepare the prunes while the stew cooks. Serve the salad dressing in a cruet for each person to pour over his wedge of lettuce.

ASSYRIAN RICE

To 1 pound of long grain rice in a bowl, add 1 tablespoon salt and water to cover the rice; let stand, covered, overnight. Drain, and bring to a boil with 1 tablespoon salt and 2 quarts boiling water in a 4-quart pan. Boil for about 6 minutes, until rice is about half cooked; drain well. Place ¼ cup butter in a covered casserole or baking pan; top with hot rice and ¼ cup more butter dotted over surface.

Cover and bake in a slow oven (300°) for about 10 minutes; stir lightly, replace cover, and continue baking for about 30 minutes more. Turn off the oven, sprinkle the rice with 1 tablespoon water, cover, and return to oven for about 5 minutes longer to steam the rice. (Rice can be reheated in a slow oven with the addition of about 2 tablespoons water.) Makes about 7 cups rice.

GLAZED PRUNES

In a deep pan place 1 pound large prunes, ¾ cup sugar, 1 thinly sliced lemon, and just enough water to cover them. Cover and bring to a boil; uncover, and continue boiling until prunes are tender and liquid is thickened and reduced, about 25 minutes. Stir often to prevent scorching. Stir in 1 tablespoon butter, and cool slightly to serve. Makes about 3 cups prunes.

OIL-LEMON DRESSING

In a blender whirl together ⅔ cup olive oil, 3 tablespoons lemon juice, and ½ teaspoon salad herbs. Makes about ¾ cup.

Ragout of Lamb

In this Basque-style ragout, you develop flavors by first browning the meat and many of the vegetables; then add liquid and bake to tenderness.

2 pounds lamb, cut for stew (about 2-inch-square
  pieces)
2 tablespoons olive oil or other salad oil
1 medium-sized onion, sliced
1 bunch carrots, whole or halved
1 bunch turnips, whole or halved
1 can (10¾ oz.) brown gravy
1 cup white table wine (or stock or water)
1 cup water
2 medium-sized tomatoes, peeled and sliced (or 2
  tablespoons tomato paste)
2 cloves garlic, minced or mashed
  Salt and pepper to taste
¼ cup finely chopped parsley

In a large frying pan, sauté the lamb pieces in olive oil until well browned on all sides. Remove the meat to a 2-quart casserole. In the same frying pan put the sliced onion and the carrots and turnips; cook, stirring frequently, over medium heat, until well browned. Put the carrots and turnips into the casserole with the meat. Drain off the fat from frying pan, leaving in the browned onions; add the brown gravy, wine, water, tomatoes, and garlic, and simmer for 20 to 30 minutes. Put through a food mill or strainer; add salt, pepper, and parsley; pour over meat and vegetables in casserole. Cover casserole and put into a moderately hot oven (375°) and cook about 1 hour, or until tender. Makes about 6 servings.

Lamb Shank Stew with Barley and Vegetables

You can cook this stew in the oven or on top of the range, as is convenient; start preparation early in the day or the day before to allow time for the meat to cool once.

½ cup pearl barley
  Water
6 lamb shanks, cracked
2 tablespoons salad oil
4 cups water
1 bay leaf
2 teaspoons salt
½ teaspoon thyme
¼ teaspoon pepper
2 medium-sized onions, thinly sliced
3 stalks celery, cut diagonally in ½-inch slices
6 carrots, cut diagonally in ½-inch slices
2 tablespoons capers

Cover barley with water and soak while lamb shanks cook. Brown lamb shanks, a few at a time, in the salad oil in a large Dutch oven or heavy pan; return all the shanks to pan and add the 4 cups water and bay leaf. Bring to a boil, then simmer over medium heat or in a moderate oven (350°) about 2½ hours, or until meat easily comes away from bones. Cool; skim fat from the broth.

Remove meat from bones, discarding bones, and return meat to broth. Drain barley and add to meat along with salt, thyme, pepper, onions, celery, carrots, and capers. Cook about 30 minutes, or until vegetables are just tender. The stew will be quite thick; if you prefer more liquid, stir in ½ to 1 cup water. Makes about 8 servings.

Idaho Venison Stew

The rich flavor of venison is especially good in a long simmered stew. This one is a simple combination of venison and vegetables. Try it with hot biscuits on a cool fall day.

2 pounds venison, cut in 1-inch cubes
4 tablespoons bacon fat
  About 3 cups water
1 teaspoon Worcestershire
1 teaspoon garlic powder
½ cup chopped onion
2 teaspoons salt
¼ teaspoon pepper
4 medium-sized potatoes
6 carrots, sliced
2 cups diced celery
4 to 6 small onions, halved
2 tablespoons flour
¼ cup cold water

Brown the venison in a large Dutch oven or heavy pan in the bacon fat, stirring to brown evenly. Add the 3 cups water, Worcestershire, garlic powder, chopped onions, salt, and pepper; cover. Simmer for about 2 hours, stirring occasionally; add more water if needed. Cut potatoes into 1-inch cubes and add along with the sliced carrots, diced celery, and halved onions to the mixture in the pan. Cook until the vegetables are tender, about 15 minutes. Thicken the gravy by adding a paste made from the flour and ¼ cup cold water. Makes 6 to 8 servings.

Green Pea Stew

A basic meatless sauce is the integral ingredient for the following four dishes (on this page and page 94). Since it takes no more time to make in fair quantity than in small amounts, prepare a full recipe. Freeze the extra portions. The sauce is also good served with hot spaghetti.

The natural sweetness of peas subtly mellows and completely alters the character of the basic meatless sauce in this dish. Tender morsels of beef make a pleasant contrast for plump juicy peas.

1½ pounds beef stew meat, cubed
¾ teaspoon salt
  2 or 3 tablespoons salad oil or olive oil
  3 cups meatless Italian gravy (recipe on this page)
  6 cups shelled fresh peas or 3 packages (10 oz. each) frozen peas

Sprinkle meat with salt. In a wide heavy pan, brown meat in oil. Add gravy and peas. Cover and simmer gently for about 1 hour and 15 minutes, or until meat is tender; stir stew occasionally. Makes 8 servings.

MEATLESS ITALIAN GRAVY:

1 cup dried mushrooms
  Hot water
3 tablespoons salad oil or olive oil
3 cups chopped parsley (about 1 bunch)
2 or 3 stalks celery, chopped
1 medium-sized onion, chopped
2 cloves garlic, minced
2-inch sprig fresh rosemary or ½ teaspoon dried rosemary
2 or 3 stems fresh thyme or ½ teaspoon dried thyme
5 small leaves fresh sage or ½ teaspoon dried sage
4 cans (8 oz. each) tomato sauce
2 cans (1 lb. each) solid pack tomatoes, chopped
1 whole red chile (chile pequin)
  Salt to taste (about 1½ teaspoons)

Place mushrooms in a small bowl and barely cover with hot water; set aside. In a large heavy pan, heat oil and add parsley, celery, onion, garlic, and herbs; cook until vegetables are soft. Stir in tomato sauce, tomatoes, and chile pequin; chop mushrooms and add with liquid. Cover and simmer slowly for 3 hours. Add salt to taste; let cool. Store in covered jars in the refrigerator up to 3 weeks; or freeze. Makes about 2½ quarts.

Pork and Olive Stew

The predominant flavor of rosemary is a characteristic part of this unusual pork entrée, but you may want to taste-test before adding the full amount of the herb. To give the dish more color, you can use half ripe and half green ripe (not pickled) olives.

    2 pounds lean pork, cut in ¾-inch cubes
    2 to 3 tablespoons salad oil or olive oil
    1-inch sprig fresh rosemary, or ¼ teaspoon dried
        rosemary (optional)
    1 clove garlic, unpeeled
    2 cups meatless Italian gravy (recipe on page 93)
    ¼ cup water
    1 can (about 7 oz.) pitted ripe or green ripe olives,
        drained
    ¾ teaspoon salt

In a heavy frying pan, brown pork in oil; include a little pork fat, if there is any. Add rosemary, garlic, gravy (see page 93), water, olives, and salt. Cover and simmer slowly for about 1 hour, or until meat is tender; stir occasionally. Spoon out and discard garlic clove. Makes 6 servings.

Veal Scallopini

Mushrooms, browned cubes of veal, and basic meatless gravy make this scallopini simple, but of excellent flavor.

    1 pound veal, cut in ½-inch cubes
    ½ teaspoon salt
      Pepper
      Flour
    2 or 3 tablespoons salad oil or olive oil
    2 cans (4 oz. each) button mushrooms, including
        liquid
    1½ cups meatless Italian gravy (recipe on
        page 93)

Season veal with salt; sprinkle with pepper and dust with flour. In a heavy frying pan, brown meat in oil. Add mushrooms, mushroom liquid, and gravy. Cover and simmer gently for about 1 hour or until meat is tender; stir occasionally. (If sauce is a little thick for your taste, thin with water or beef broth.) Makes 4 servings.

Castiglioni Stew

This savory stew, like all good stews, is even better reheated. The sauce is plentiful and not too thick, so it's a good idea to serve the stew in bowls, along with crusty French bread or crisp bread sticks.

    1½ pounds beef stew meat, cubed
     3 tablespoons salad oil or olive oil
     2 cups meatless Italian gravy (recipe on
         page 93)
     1 can (8 oz.) tomato sauce
     1 can (14 oz.) chicken broth
     3 medium-sized potatoes, cubed
     4 carrots, cut in chunks
     2 or 3 stalks celery, cut in chunks
     1 can (about 7 oz.) pitted ripe or green ripe
         olives, drained
     1 can (4 oz.) mushrooms and liquid (if desired)
       Salt (about 1 teaspoon)

In a large heavy pan, brown meat in oil. Remove meat from pan and add gravy, tomato sauce, and broth. Let simmer for 10 minutes. Return meat to sauce along with potatoes, carrots, celery, olives, mushrooms, and mushroom liquid. Add salt to taste. Cover and cook slowly for about 2 hours, stirring occasionally. Makes 8 generous servings.

PHOTOGRAPHERS: Glenn M. Christiansen, pages 8, 18, 25, 35, 41, 51, 74, 89;
Darrow M. Watt, pages 4, 11, 13, 15, 16, 22, 28, 36, 45, 54, 57, 61, 68, 71, 80, 84.